THE IMMORTAL TEN

THE IMMORTAL TEN

The definitive account of the 1927 tragedy and its
legacy at Baylor University

Todd Copeland

BAYLOR UNIVERSITY PRESS

Cover Design by Pamela Poll; Book Design by Diane Smith

All interior and cover photographs are used by permission and
courtesy of The Texas Collection, Baylor University; the *Round-
Up*, Baylor University; Baylor Photography, Baylor University;
James Powell; the *Austin American-Statesman*; and individual
photographers Todd Copeland and Rod Aydelotte.

Library of Congress Cataloging-in-Publication Data

Copeland, Todd, 1968-
  The immortal ten : the definitive account of the 1927 tragedy that
stunned the state of Texas and left a lasting mark on Baylor
University / Todd Copeland.
     p. cm.
  Includes bibliographical references.
  ISBN-13: 978-1-932792-90-4 (pbk. : alk. paper)
  1. Round Rock (Tex.)--History--20th century 2. Bus accidents--
Texas--Round Rock--History--20th century. 3. Railroad accidents-
-Texas--Round Rock--History--20th century. 4. Traffic
fatalities--Texas--Round Rock--History--20th century. 5. College
students--Texas--Death--History--20th century. 6. College ath-
letes--Texas--Death--History--20th century. 7. College students--
Texas--Biography. 8. College athletes--Texas--Biography. 9.
Baylor University--Biography. 10. Baylor University--History--
20th century. I. Title.

  F394.R68C67 2006
  976.4'289--dc22

                                          2006030283

TABLE OF CONTENTS

PREFACE

This book began as a feature story in the *Baylor Line*, the
magazine of the Baylor Alumni Association which I have
edited since 1998. My goals in writing that story for the
winter 2002 issue of the *Line* were simple. First, I wanted
to provide a dependable history of the bus-train collision
in Round Rock that took the lives of ten Baylor students—most of them prominent athletes—on January
22, 1927. Second, I aspired to tell the story of the accident and its aftermath in a way that would engage readers by capturing the sights and sounds of the events and
bringing to life the young men involved.

Those goals grew out of specific circumstances. As
the seventy-fifth anniversary of the accident approached,
I surveyed the materials previously written about the
Immortal Ten as part of the magazine staff's process of
determining how the *Line* would cover the anniversary.
Although honoring the Immortal Ten had been a long-
standing and central tradition at Baylor University, I discovered that the stories published in the decades
following the tragedy were remarkably incomplete—lim-

ited to brief historical columns, similarly brief personal accounts by Baylor alumni of that era, and superficially researched articles in newspapers that committed factual errors and perpetuated certain suspect legends that had grown up around the accident.

Of course, such stories served a purpose in their time, and their writers were well intentioned; if nothing else, they helped keep the story alive. But the fact that no one had ever thoroughly told the story of this important piece of Baylor's heritage in a narrative format, based on research in primary sources, struck me as a regrettable gap in the institution's recorded history. I resolved to fill that gap.

When America suffered the terrorist attacks of September 11, 2001, I was deep into researching the story on the Immortal Ten. Becoming immersed in the lives of the ten Baylor students who died in that horrible accident had been a somber enough enterprise. But after the terrorist attacks, I found working on this story to be even more emotionally difficult. Between reading the morning newspaper and exploring historical archives, my days were filled with what seemed like an unending involvement with death and grief.

Much of my sorrow was connected to the lives of William Winchester and Robert Hannah Jr., two of the Baylor basketball players killed in the collision. Through the invaluable help of Ellen Kuniyuki Brown at Baylor's Texas Collection, my research had uncovered a wealth of letters relating to the Winchester and Hannah families that pulled me into the young men's close friendship, which had begun during their years together at Waco High School, and brought home the sadness of their passing.

Winchester's wit and vitality came alive in the letters he wrote to Hannah during the hot summer months preceding what would be their last year in school. Winchester provided colorful accounts of his long hours working at an ice factory, and he kept his friend up to date on the activities of their teammates. Hannah's family had recently moved to St. Louis, and the logistics and expectations surrounding Winchester's planned trip from Waco to visit his friend in that distant metropolis were frequent topics in their correspondence.

But the letters that Winchester's mother wrote to Hannah's mother in the months after their sons' deaths moved me the most. Katherine Winchester told Mary Jane Hannah that she desperately needed to share her grief with someone because her dual roles at home as a wife and a mother—William's twin brother and younger brother were both Baylor students at the time—required her to be a pillar of strength. "I do my grieving by myself," she wrote. The bereaved mothers did their best to comfort one another in a succession of letters through those dark days.

I eventually discovered that researching and writing the story of the Immortal Ten helped mitigate the sorrow and anxiety I felt in the wake of September 11. I came to see how renewal could follow a time of tremendous grief. I saw how the crash's twelve survivors went on to make a difference in their communities and professions with their spared lives. And I saw how the ten victims, through their commemoration, inspired a life-affirming tradition that still continues at Baylor.

Although the article I wrote was well received by the *Line*'s readers, I was left with several nagging concerns following its publication. Constrained by space and a deadline, I had not been able to tell the story in as much detail as I desired or to follow all possible lines of research to their conclusion. In the following years, I set about gathering more information through further archival research and by locating and interviewing additional relatives and friends of the students involved in the bus-train crash—and then assimilating the new material into the narrative. I hope the end result of that extended work is a book that will serve Baylor University well into the future by preserving a remarkable episode in the school's history.

*

Before beginning the story of the Immortal Ten, I would like to make a few comments about two aspects of this book. The first has to do with the story's narrative structure, and the second has to do with the editorial practices underlying the narrative's content.

Because this is a story about an accident that took only a few seconds to occur, the narrative's structure heavily depends upon what came before and after the crash. Figuratively speaking, the structure is that of an hourglass. Everything that the twenty-two passengers had been before noon on January 22, 1927, was brought to a point of definition during the calamity's narrow passage in time. Conversely, for those who survived—as well as for the Baylor community in general—everything that followed the accident would be informed by its expanding consequences. Accordingly, I have devoted considerable space in the first section of this book to describing the personalities, relationships, and activities of the men on the bus, and I have filled the last section with accounts of the accident's long aftermath and of the lives that the survivors went on to lead.

Concerning my editorial practices in telling the story of the Immortal Ten, I would like to note, for the sake of authorial transparency, that I have reconstructed a few scenes using details that are not strictly factual. One such scene occurs at the beginning, when the athletic bus is readied for travel and boarded by the team. However, in all instances these reconstructions are in keeping with general information as provided by several Baylor alumni of that era whom I interviewed and what I hope are reasonable inferences from the circumstances of a given situation. I have taken these liberties in the interest of providing a compelling, seamless narrative history and have engaged in such acts of poetic license as infrequently as possible and only when the details of a critical scene were scant or nonexistent in primary sources. The overwhelming majority of details presented in this story are drawn from primary sources—corroborated if possible—and adhere tightly to the set of information reported by journalists of the day and statements by the people directly involved in the events recounted.

LIST OF ILLUSTRATIONS

DEPARTING BAYLOR

The weather was raw in Waco that Saturday morning — January 22, 1927. A norther was sweeping across Texas, and the temperature would drop toward the freezing point as the day passed. Mist and fog — the lingering effects of the previous night's intermittent rain — deepened the late-January chill.

On the north side of Baylor University's Carroll Field, a broad-shouldered freshman named Joe Potter drove the athletic bus out of its large tin barn. He wheeled the vehicle around in front of the two-story athletic building, which featured a grandstand on the side facing the playing field where the school's football, baseball, and track teams competed. Potter had come to Baylor from nearby West and looked every part the athlete he was; his five-foot-nine frame was lean and muscular, and his high cheekbones and dark hair framed a face that could go cold with intensity. That fall, playing on the freshman football team, he had been an outstanding halfback who could also punt the ball deep down the field.

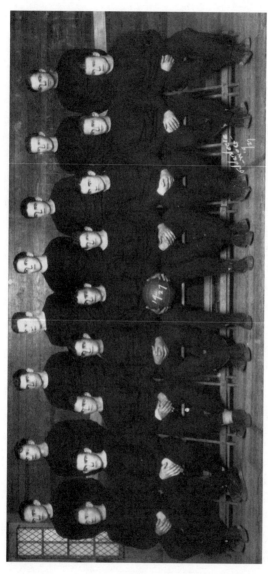

The 1927 Baylor varsity basketball squad. Pictured on the top row are (l-r, with asterisks designating those killed):
Ira Dryden, Fred Acree Jr., John Kane, Cecil Bean, Robert Hailey*, Shelton Gillam, Gordon Barry, and Coach Ralph
Wolf. Pictured on the bottom row are (l-r): Willis Murray*, William Winchester*, Sam Dillow*, Keifer Strickland,
Louis Slade, James Walker* Robert Hannah Jr.*, Clyde "Abe" Kelley*, and Weir Washam.
Photograph courtesy of The Texas Collection, Baylor University.

But being an athlete didn't mean living a life of ease and privilege. Potter was like many regular Baylor students who, lacking the means to pay for all the necessary expenses, had to work their way through school. His job, quite simply, was to drive the bus. The new football coach and athletic director, Morley Jennings, had given the freshman that assignment at the beginning of the school year. And so, during the fall quarter, Potter had dutifully driven the freshman and varsity football squads to their games across the state. Between trips he kept the bus clean, full of gas, and in good operating condition.

That Saturday, the trip to Austin—where Baylor's varsity basketball team would play the University of Texas in the evening—promised to be just another day on the road, though a cold and muddy one.

Once Potter had steered the bus between the temporary chapel building, where the basketball team practiced and played its games, and the front of the athletic building, Ed Gooch began loading the vehicle with the team's equipment. He stowed some gear inside by the driver's seat and secured bags to a rack on top, at the rear of the bus.

Like Potter, Gooch had been on the freshman football team that fall, playing tackle, and earned his keep working as an assistant in the athletic department. One of his main duties was to issue equipment to athletes in the check room, but he also cut the grass at Carroll Field, kept the track clean, and performed other odd jobs. He was old for a freshman—one day from turning twenty-one—and stood a few inches above most of his classmates. His long face had a mature, friendly look to it, with heavily lidded eyes and a narrow jaw. His role that

Merle Dudley, a second-year law student from Abilene, was a Baylor yell leader. Photograph courtesy of The Texas Collection, Baylor University.

Saturday was to serve as the equipment manager on the trip. His older brother, Aubrey "Tiny" Gooch, was a football star at the University of Texas, and so there was a promising likelihood that the two would cross paths at the game.

With the equipment loaded and everything readied for travel, the bus idled amid the parking lot's puddles as, checked off one by one, the team boarded the bus. Coach Ralph Wolf followed the last player on board and took a seat up front. A glance back showed the bus filled to capacity. In addition to the team's members, six young men were traveling to Austin in supporting roles. One of them was Dave Cheavens, a sophomore from El Paso, who served as the managing editor of the campus newspaper, the *Daily Lariat*. Another was second-year law student Merle Dudley, from Abilene—the only one of Baylor's four yell leaders who had agreed to make the trip. "I will have to be the Baylor rooting section tonight," he would tell a fellow traveler later in the trip, "but I guess they will be able to hear me." Including Potter, seated behind the wheel, the men on board totaled twenty-one.

Purchased in 1924 from the REO Motor Car Company, the parlor bus featured a low, blocky cabin that measured about eight feet in width and twenty-five feet in length. A narrow aisle divided four rows of wicker chairs into two columns, with two seats on either side. At the back, four more chairs formed a fifth row that was bordered by emergency doors, which swung open toward the front. The chairs were anchored to the wooden floor, and at each window a set of cloth drapes hung between two horizontal curtain rods, providing protection from the sun or simply privacy from the out-

Baylor's basketball team traveled to competitions in a twenty-one passenger parlor bus that was purchased in 1924 from the REO Motor Car Co. This photograph was taken during the 1925–26 school year. Photograph from the Round-Up, Baylor University.

side world. Stenciled on the side of the bus were the words "Baylor University, Waco, Texas."

As the bus pulled away from Carroll Field, leaving the campus's landmark towers of Burleson Hall and the Main Building behind, the group was beginning a journey whose story would be told into the next century. It would not, however, be a tale of glory on the basketball court. In fact, the scheduled game would never be contested. What awaited those on the bus was tragedy; almost half of the passengers were only hours away from horribly sudden and violent deaths in what at the time would be the worst bus-train accident in Texas history.

Within days, the collision's victims would become known as "The Immortal Ten," their individual lives linked together by a collective mourning that spread across the state of Texas and beyond. For those who would survive, the crash would prove to be a defining moment in their lives. And for Baylor University, what occurred on January 22, 1927, and during the following days would leave an immediate and lasting mark upon the university's character.

—2—

THE BEST OF HOPES

Among the starters slated for that night's game against Texas was twenty-year-old Robert Hannah Jr., whom family members and friends called Bob. He was a slightly built guard with a high forehead and protruding ears who was valued for his fighting spirit and defensive skills. Unlike many of his teammates, who played multiple sports, Hannah was a basketball specialist. The year before, as a sophomore, he had worked his way into the starting lineup. Now that he was an upperclassman, his talent and single-minded focus had established him in a leadership role.

Hannah had grown up in Waco, but his family had relocated the previous spring to St. Louis where his father, an engineer, had taken a new job. Instead of enjoying the support of nearby parents, Hannah found himself having to maintain ties through correspondence. "I think I am making pretty good grades," the business student had written his parents in early December from the Greer House, where he was a boarder. "As for my

Robert Hannah Jr., a junior from Waco, was a starting guard on the basketball team. Photograph courtesy of The Texas Collection, Baylor University.

girl in Hillsboro, I haven't seen her since Nov. 14th. I hear from her occasionally through the mail. I have been too busy to run around any." He had, however, recently enjoyed the opportunity to see more of his parents. During the Christmas break he had traveled back home to St. Louis, and Mrs. Hannah had arrived in Waco a week before the game against Texas to spend time with her only son, her brother, and the family's friends.

Although hundreds of miles had separated Hannah from his parents during the fall, he saw his close friend William Winchester on a regular, if not daily, basis. Winchester was a handsome young man, with a long face and a strong chin. He was an excellent student, majoring in history and French, who ranked in the top 10 percent

William Winchester, a senior from Waco, substituted at center and guard.
Photograph courtesy of The Texas Collection, Baylor University.

of his senior class, and he was also a leader of the local order of the Boy Scouts.

A year older than Hannah, Winchester was a substitute center on the basketball team and, like his friend, had come to Baylor from Waco High School, where he had played football as well as basketball. Indeed, as a senior he had lettered on the school's football team that won the state championship. Winchester and his twin brother, Robert, had entered Baylor in the fall of 1923 and had played together on the freshman, or "Cub," football team. Their younger brother, Albert, had followed them to Baylor two years later.

In college, Winchester had tasted more athletic success, albeit mostly from the sidelines; during his sophomore year, he had played as a back-up center on the varsity football team that won the Southwest Conference (SWC) title, and he had been a second-string member of the varsity basketball team. Disappointingly, his junior year had brought no improvement to his status as a multi-sport substitute. And so, during the previous summer — while working twelve-hour days at an ice factory in Waco, for which he rose at 4:15 in the morning — Winchester had soberly evaluated his prospects for his final year at Baylor.

"I am in fine shape at present as I work hard, sleep and eat plenty, and cut out all candy and cold drinks," he had written Hannah on August 10, 1926, just prior to visiting him and his family in St. Louis. "I am almost ready to play basketball right now. I got a card . . . the other day inviting me to come to [football] training camp Sept. 10. For a while I thought of going, for football has a sort of fascination which nothing else gives, even if it is hard work and plenty of it. But for several reasons I finally decided not to go. I did not want to quit my job that early. Also I believe I have a better chance in basket-ball and I would be unable to get in shape for the court game if I came out for football."

Though Winchester hadn't achieved the kind of personal success he undoubtedly desired as an athlete, his passion for Baylor athletics had remained ardent and his own perspective had stayed unwaveringly optimistic. "Here's hoping September rolls around sooner than ever this year and that Baylor wins the flag in all *three* sports," he had written Hannah earlier that summer. "It's a cinch in basketball, is it not, old rear guard Hannah? Why of course it is!"

During the fall and early winter Baylor's athletic fortunes had failed to measure up to Winchester's hopes, though they hadn't been entirely lackluster. Under new head coach Jennings, the football team had finished second in the SWC with a 3-1-1 record, including a big 20-7 Homecoming win over Texas A&M on October 30.

That game, however, had been marred by tragedy. Playing at Waco's Cotton Palace field before a crowd numbering about twenty-five thousand, the Bears were leading the Aggies by a score of 13–7 when a halftime brawl on the field resulted in what would prove the next morning to be a fatal injury to a Texas A&M senior, Charles Sessums. As part of the halftime entertainment, Baylor students drove a green-and-gold-decorated Ford Model T flat-bed truck around the field. In the back stood several Baylor women, each dressed in the fashion of particular years in which Baylor had soundly beaten A&M—and each bearing a sign showing the respective year's score.

When the vehicle passed by the Texas A&M section, three cadets from the all-male school jumped over the grandstand's fence and ran to the truck, where they pulled off some of the women and attempted to overpower the driver. Members of Baylor's freshman football team, seated on the sideline near the varsity squad, rushed to the women's defense. Immediately, Baylor and A&M students swarmed the field and threw themselves into a chaotic fight, some swinging pieces of the fence's wooden railing while others grabbed wooden folding chairs from the edge of the field. The Aggie band broke into "The Star-Spangled Banner," which eventually brought the cadets to attention and ended the violence.

The A&M students who started the fight later claimed they had thought the Baylor women were actually men dressed like coeds. In the aftermath, the two schools' presidents agreed to a moratorium on football competition between Baylor and Texas A&M that eventually lasted four years—enough time to allow a generation of students to graduate.

Just prior to the Christmas break, several members of that Baylor football team—Clyde "Abe" Kelley, Robert Hailey, Louis Slade, Weir Washam, Fred Acree Jr., Keifer Strickland, Sam Dillow, and John Kane—had traded in their helmets and cleats for basketball jerseys and hightops. It was an era when sports' seasons were relatively brief and didn't necessarily demand specialized off-season training. A number of Baylor's stars were all-around athletes, and the rosters for a given year's football, basketball, and baseball teams featured many of the same names.

By late January 1927, the success in basketball that Winchester had predicted would be "a cinch" had proven to be anything but. Based on their competitive 1926 season and the fact that all five starters were returning, the Bears had been considered one of the teams favored to win the SWC championship, but they had lost their first three games in conference play—all on their home court, no less. Without the demands of a shot clock, basketball games of that day were usually low-scoring affairs due to the time-consuming, keep-away passing strategy used by the team in the lead. Four days before the Bears left town to play Texas, TCU had beaten Baylor by a score of 31 to 24.

Coach Wolf had debated whether or not to make the trip to Austin for that night's game against the Longhorns.

Ralph Wolf was serving in his first year as the head coach of the varsity basketball team. Photograph from the Round-Up, Baylor University.

With his wife in the final days of her pregnancy, he was predictably reluctant to leave Waco. But earlier that morning he had called his boss, Morley Jennings, to say he would travel with the team after all.

Though Wolf was a somewhat mild-mannered man, given to wearing bow ties and sporting coat pocket handkerchiefs, he had a strong competitive spirit. Prior to graduating from Baylor in 1921, he had lettered in football, basketball, and track, setting conference records in the 100-, 220-, and 440-yard dashes. This was his first year as the varsity basketball team's head coach—after having worked for the past five years as a trainer for the football team, head track coach, and coach of the freshman basketball team—and this was his squad's first road game of the 1927 season. The Bears' losing streak had begun with a 22–15 loss to Texas. The team wanted revenge and an opportunity to show greater offensive power than they had exhibited in their first contest against the Longhorns. More simply, they needed a win. It was the kind of game that a first-year head coach didn't miss.

—3—

IN THE COMPANY OF FRIENDS

The friendship between Winchester and Hannah was just one example of the strong bonds that linked members of the team. Keifer Strickland, a junior who started at forward and led the team in scoring, was also close to Hannah and his family, having lived in Waco before attending high school in Hazard, Kentucky.

The most well-known local boys on the team were Clyde "Abe" Kelley and Weir Washam, who had been friends since childhood. The Baylor juniors had been two of Waco High's best all-around athletes, playing on the football team that in 1922 won the school's first state championship. That fall, in the Homecoming win over Texas A&M, Washam and Kelley had both scored touchdowns.

Kelley had long been the darling of the local sports press, which had given him his nickname of Abe. His genuine friendliness and boyish good looks, even at the age of twenty-three, made him a favorite with classmates

Clyde "Abe" Kelley, a junior from Waco, was a substitute forward on the basketball team. Photograph courtesy of The Texas Collection, Baylor University.

as well. Physically, he was solid muscle—broad-chested and of medium height. During his sophomore year at Baylor, he had lettered on the football, basketball, and baseball teams. His outstanding play as a halfback and punter during the fall had earned him all-conference honors, and the football team had recently elected him to serve as captain next year.

Kelley came from a large family, with four brothers and four sisters, and financial circumstances required him to work for the Waco fire department for pay and lodging. He lived at Station No. 4, located about two blocks beyond campus at Fifth Street and James Avenue. Kelley was studying business administration

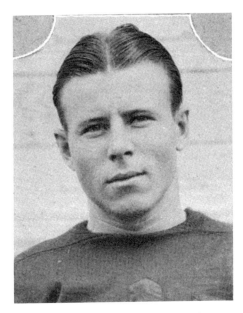

Weir Washam, a friend of Kelley's since childhood, was a junior who played as a back-up on the basketball team. Photograph from the Round-Up, Baylor University.

and commerce and was active in the J. W. Speight Masonic lodge, but the constraints of his many activities didn't stop him from spending time with his girlfriend, a sophomore named Dorris Roberts, whom he had begun dating in high school. Recently, however, they had quarreled, and when he had tried to make up with her the day before the basketball game against Texas, she had declined to talk to him.

Washam was a year younger than Kelley, and he was physically smaller than his friend. But what he lacked in size was more than offset by his skill and competitiveness. His face featured a broad forehead and close-set eyes that could give him an intense appearance, especially when they were staring out of a football helmet. Washam dabbled in basketball, playing as a substitute, but his real passion was football. However, his success on the gridiron had come more slowly than his friend's. Washam had been forced to play on the freshman football team during his first two years at Baylor, having been ruled ineligible for the varsity as a sophomore. But during the fall of 1926 he had emerged as a force at quarterback. Known as "Wee Willie," he was tremendously elusive when he had the ball in his hands. His older brother, Hyams, had preceded him as a Baylor student and was then serving as director of the Baylor Band, so during the fall there had always been two Washams performing when the Bears took the field for a home game.

Kelley and Washam were part of a sizeable contingent of Waco High graduates who in recent years had helped to firmly establish Baylor football as a formidable program, as well as providing talent to the school's other sports. What these athletes brought to Baylor from Waco High was a champion's mindset; they were used to winning, they knew the dedication and determination required to win, and they expected to continuing winning.

Their mentor was Paul Tyson, who had begun his football coaching career at Waco High in 1913. Under his leadership, the Waco High Tigers had quickly become successful. By the early 1920s, they were a true powerhouse. In 1921, Waco High went undefeated, but the team wasn't able to play for the official state championship because the school had yet to join the University Interscholastic League (UIL). The next year, having joined the UIL, Waco High compiled a record of 11-0-1—beating teams by such scores as 119-0 and 100-0—and defeated Abilene for the school's first state title. In 1923, the team won its first eleven contests before losing to Abilene, 3-0, in the state championship game. Remarkably, Abilene's points were the only ones scored against Waco High that year. In contrast, the Tigers amassed a total of 636 points against their opponents.

Many of Tyson's top athletes chose to pursue their collegiate careers at Baylor, which in 1922 won its first SWC championship in football. Playing for the Bears, the Waco boys' winning ways continued. When Baylor won its second SWC football title, in 1924, seven of the starters were Waco High alumni, including such standouts as Homer "Bear" Walker, Sam Coates, and Jack Sisco, and several of the substitutes, such as Winchester, were former Tigers.

During the fall of 1924, while their varsity counterparts were achieving glory, the most recent Waco High football products to enroll at Baylor were playing on the freshman squad. In addition to Kelley and Washam, they included Louis Slade and Boody Johnson, who was regarded by many as the greatest player in Texas high school football history. These young men had been integral members of those remarkable Waco High teams of 1921, 1922, and 1923, but as Baylor freshmen they were relegated to scrimmaging the varsity team and waiting for their chance.

Two years later, those freshmen had become juniors and legitimate Baylor stars in their own right. The camaraderie and culture of athletic excellence they had carried with them from Waco High had brought increased

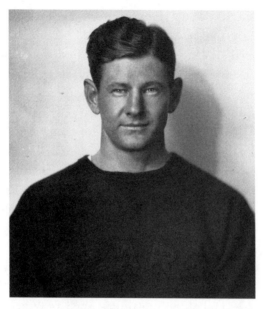

James Walker, a junior from Gatesville. played forward on the basketball team. Photograph courtesy of The Texas Collection, Baylor University.

competitiveness to all the sports in which they partici-
pated. It wasn't naive optimism, then, that had prompted
Winchester the previous summer to entertain hopes that
Baylor would win "the flag in all *three* sports." It was an
expectation of success based on experience.

As was the case with the young men from Waco, a
shared hometown connected James Walker and Willis
Murray, who had graduated together from Gatesville
High School.

Known around campus as Jim or Jimmie, Walker
was a sturdily built twenty-three-year-old junior with a
head of thick dark hair and a rough-hewn quality to his
face. He came from a large family of modest means that

Willis Murray, a junior from Gatesville, was the team's manager and a substitute guard. Photograph courtesy of The Texas Collection, Baylor University.

included four older brothers and two younger sisters. Success as an athlete had opened the door for him to attend college, and he was making the most of the opportunity by studying business administration and commerce. At Gatesville, Walker had been a multi-year letterman in football, basketball, and track, and he also had played tennis and baseball. Nicknamed "Tuff," he played halfback in football and was praised as "a sure tackler" and "a side stepper and broken field runner." As the captain and right forward on the basketball team his senior year, during which Gatesville went 16-2 with several lopsided wins, he scored a total of 279 points for the season.

After playing on Baylor's freshman football and basketball teams, Walker had emerged as a genuine talent. The previous year, as a sophomore, he had made the varsity squad in football and had won a starting position at forward on the varsity basketball team due to his dead-aim passing skills. He also had earned a reputation as the "iron man" of the track team by running the mile in less than four and a half minutes and winning the mile and two-mile runs in a dual meet against Rice the previous spring after only a week's training. But he wasn't one to boast. In contrast to most of his teammates, who were a prank-playing, typically outgoing group of young men, he was a quiet presence in a room—friendly, but content to keep his thoughts to himself.

Much of Willis Murray's interest in basketball stemmed from his friendship with Walker during their days together at Gatesville High, where Murray's admiration of Walker had fueled his successful efforts to become a teammate during their senior year. After entering Baylor at the age of sixteen, Murray had played on the freshman basketball team. As a sophomore, he had been a back-up guard on the varsity squad, though he never made it onto the court during a game.

Murray was still youthful-looking as an eighteen-year-old junior working toward both a bachelor of arts and a law degree. Somewhat short and fair-skinned, with reddish-blond hair, he was a personable young man who often could be found hanging around the Victrola at the nearby drug store or spending time with his girlfriend. During his high school years, he and his five siblings had filled up their family's modest home, located on a farm about two miles outside Gatesville. His father co-owned a grocery store on the town square and supplemented his income by selling milk from his dairy cows to the Borden Company. During his first years studying in Waco, Murray had one day received word from his younger sister Nina that their father was planning to sell his beloved saddle pony, Snip. With Willis away at college, the pony was no longer being ridden and had become, in the father's eyes, a needless expense. Murray set out on foot for the thirty-five-mile journey to Gatesville, determined to save Snip. Having learned of his rash action, the family took off in their car and met him halfway. Murray's appeals won the day, and the pony happily spent the remainder of his years at the farm. The previous fall, another of his younger sisters, Edna, had followed him to Baylor, and now the family had even more reason to make an occasional train trip to Waco.

Murray had settled into a peripheral role on the varsity basketball team, primarily serving as manager but ready to come in at guard if needed. After having been a boarder in a house owned by a Gatesville friend's mother, Murray was enjoying rooming in Brooks Hall and working in The Campus Shop on the first floor. He was right in the middle of campus life, happy to have as friends and teammates the young men who surrounded him in the bus.

—4—

ON THE BUS

The passengers settled into their wicker chairs as they left Waco, around 8:30 a.m., and prepared for what, even in good weather, would be a long ride. The hundred-mile trip to Austin routinely took more than three hours, with ninety-degree turns around farms, especially in Bell County, interrupting a vehicle's normal speed of thirty-five to forty miles per hour.

Within the bus's close quarters, the young men talked or stared out at the countryside passing by as they made their way south. Keifer Strickland and senior substitute Gordon Barry sat directly behind the driver. To their right, across the narrow aisle, were Coach Wolf and Louis Slade, the team's captain and lanky starting center.

When Wolf looked back to survey his charges, he saw the second row occupied, from left to right, by Cecil Bean, equipment manager Ed Gooch, *Lariat* managing editor Dave Cheavens, and John Kane. Bean was a junior from Grapeland who substituted at center, while

Kane, a junior majoring in zoology, had come from St. Louis to study at his father's alma mater. Even though Kane hadn't risen above back-up status on the varsity football and basketball squads, his teammates regarded him as an ideal physical specimen. Others agreed. A favorite anecdote about Kane maintained that when the football players were getting their physicals before a recent season, the doctor examining Kane suddenly summoned a colleague. "Look at this young man—he's perfectly built!" he reportedly told the other doctor.

On the bus's third row, behind Cheavens and Kane, sat starting forward Jim Walker and Wesley Bradshaw, who was traveling with the team as an invited guest. The former Baylor quarterback had captained the football team to the school's first conference championship, in 1922, and was considered one of the SWC's greatest athletes, having won letters in four sports—football, basketball, baseball, and track. During that fabled 1922 season, he had scored five touchdowns in a 60-13 win over Arkansas and had played with his shoulder in a cast in the championship-clinching 24-0 defeat of SMU. In addition to his quarterbacking exploits, Bradshaw had served as the team's punter and place-kicker, adding four field goals and twenty-three extra points to his fourteen touchdowns for a total of 119 points for the year. He had gone on to play professionally in the early years of the National Football League and had been a teammate of the legendary Jim Thorpe on the Rock Island Independents in 1924. Bradshaw had just wrapped up a season with the Buffalo Rangers.

Rounding out the third row and occupying chairs on the fourth row were Willis Murray, starting guard Bob

Hannah, William Winchester, and Fred Acree Jr., a Waco sophomore who played as a substitute in football and basketball. Also among the group was the team's official scorekeeper, Jack Castellaw. A senior from Ennis studying business administration and commerce, Castellaw was the only son of a prosperous family. He had wavy blond hair and blue eyes and was known as a snappy dresser. During his years at Baylor he had been a frequent traveler with the basketball team. His eagerness to attend the game against Texas was so strong that he had decided to defer until the next weekend a trip back home to receive the first degree in Masonry.

Jack Castellaw, a senior from Ennis, was the basketball team's official scorekeeper. Photograph courtesy of The Texas Collection, Baylor University.

Sam Dillow, a junior from Fort Worth, was a starting guard for the Bears. Photograph courtesy of The Texas Collection, Baylor University.

Sitting together on the back row were Abe Kelley and Weir Washam, with Washam stationed next to the bus's right emergency door. To Kelley's left sat Sam Dillow and Robert Hailey. The team's other starting guard, Dillow was a junior business administration major from Fort Worth whose parents had attended Baylor. He had been the captain of the 1926 basketball team, and he also played wing in football and first base in baseball for the Bears. Less than a week away from turning twenty-two, he had written his mother a few days earlier to say that, following a game against TCU on the upcoming Wednesday, he would remain in Fort Worth to celebrate his birthday at home.

Robert Hailey, a sophomore from Lott, substituted at guard on the basketball team. Photograph courtesy of The Texas Collection, Baylor University.

Hailey also played football, having won a starting position at end the previous fall. On the basketball team, he substituted at guard. He was a sophomore from nearby Lott, where he had been the captain of the basketball and football teams. When passing out letterman's sweaters, Lott's football coach had described Hailey as the player around whom he had built his team. The first of his family to attend college, he was known as "Smilin' Bob" because of his ready grin and winsome personality. He lived in what was known as the Haunted House — a large home at 1305 Washington Avenue, several blocks away from Baylor, in which a group of athletes resided. A head of combed-back, slightly curly hair framed his broad face and high forehead.

In addition to common hometowns, the web of relationships that connected the students on the bus included other strands—such as shared residences. At least six of the young men—Dillow, Hannah, Dudley, Castellaw, Gooch, and Acree—were boarders at the Greer House at 1410 South Fifth Street. And Walker, Murray, and Cheavens had rooms in Brooks Hall.

Another connecting strand was membership in the Baylor Chamber of Commerce, a student-run organization that served Baylor through a range of activities, most of them relating to athletics. The group's efforts included helping to recruit athletes, organizing intramural competition in football, track, golf, and tennis, creating "Good Will Week" during the previous fall to precede Homecoming, hosting football banquets, and even buying uniforms for Baylor's band and yell leaders to wear at football games. The organization began in 1919 as the Young Men's Business League before changing its name in 1920, and over the years many of Baylor's prominent athletes and other campus leaders had been members. Such was still the case, with Dillow, Kelley, Kane, and Strickland belonging to the Chamber of Commerce. The previous Tuesday, Hailey had been elected to join the group, and he was to be initiated the following week.

The men traveling to Austin that Saturday were certainly a varied lot—in age, background, and personality. Their hometowns were scattered across the state and beyond, from small rural communities to big cities. And the players' respective talents had sorted the men into different ranks, from starters to substitutes, while others on board had connected themselves to the team in supporting roles. But despite the differences between them—and running beneath all the connections they either had brought with them or had formed in recent years—the passengers had two fundamental things in common: Baylor had brought them together on one campus, and basketball had brought them together on one bus.

—5—

THE COLLISION

When the bus reached Temple, the passengers up front were surprised to see a familiar face alongside the highway. It was Ivey Foster Jr., a freshman football and basketball player who had been given the job of assistant sports editor of the *Lariat* a week earlier. He was a dark-haired nineteen-year-old with a cleft chin who wore glasses featuring circular lenses and dark rims.

Foster was hitchhiking to Austin to catch the game and go on a date prior to visiting his family in Taylor, located just north of Austin. A businessman from Mexia had picked him up in Waco that morning and had taken him as far as Temple. A lonely figure out in the cold, miserable weather, Foster was clearly in need of charity. Potter pulled the bus over to the side of the road, and the freshman gamely found a perch on the running board since there were no seats available on the crowded bus. After several miles, Ed Gooch attracted his classmate's attention and said, "Come in here and take my seat.

You'll freeze to death out there." Foster thankfully took Gooch's place behind Coach Wolf, and Gooch fit himself into the looser arrangement of seats on the back row. The bus's occupants now numbered twenty-two.

By the time the team reached Round Rock, the trip was three and a half hours old and there were still twenty-two miles to go. It had been raining intermittently, and mud was splattered across the bus's windshield and side windows, which were blurry with mist. In the right rear corner of the bus, Washam had lowered his window so that he and Gooch, while keeping a lookout for the coach, could chew tobacco and spit outside. Up front, Joe Potter was busy driving and trying, somewhat

Ivey Foster Jr., a freshman from Taylor, was assistant sports editor of the Daily Lariat, *the student newspaper.*
Photograph courtesy of The Texas Collection, Baylor University.

awkwardly, to keep the windshield clear. The wipers required hands-on attention, with successive turns of the wrist bringing them back and forth across the glass.

Potter drove through the downtown district and turned left off Main Street between the post office and a filling station, heading south down the highway. Some of the students up front began talking about Sam Bass, the infamous nineteenth-century train robber who died from wounds received in a gunfight that had occurred only a few blocks away. Despite the chatter, Cecil Bean was sleeping soundly next to Foster. Across the aisle and one row back, Bradshaw was reading a magazine. Louis Slade asked his coach the time and learned it was a few minutes past noon.

Meanwhile, Coach Wolf had begun scanning the road ahead, where he knew the highway crossed a set of

This Diagram Shows the Events Leading Up to the Fatal Crash

This drawing of the crash site in Round Rock ran in the January 23, 1927, edition of the Austin American-Statesman. *Courtesy of the* Austin American-Statesman.

train tracks. The road ran downhill to the tracks and then continued up a slight rise. The railroad crossing was well known to travelers, but it was nevertheless an open grade crossing that required caution. Potter was unfamiliar with that section of the highway and hadn't been forewarned about the crossing. Trying to negotiate muddy holes and pools of water on the road, he was driving slowly at about fifteen to twenty miles per hour. But he was still having trouble seeing through the mud-splattered windshield. Wolf also found it difficult to see what he was looking for, as several buildings blocked the view of the tracks to the west until the bus was about two hundred feet from the crossing. Closer to the tracks, the westward view was further blocked by a small tool house as well as a boxcar and some passenger cars on a siding.

What Wolf couldn't see was that the "Sunshine Special"—a northbound passenger train belonging to the International-Great Northern Railroad Company, which was part of the Missouri Pacific Lines—was rapidly approaching from the west. The train was running slightly behind schedule, and the engineer, Sid Crews, was attempting to make up for lost time by running the engine at about sixty miles per hour through the flat stretch of land around Round Rock. As he neared the crossing, he pulled the whistle cord and held it to announce his imminent passage. He saw nothing but clear tracks ahead.

No one on the bus heard the train's whistle. When Coach Wolf suddenly saw the speeding engine flash into view on his right, he shouted, "Look out!" The bus was only a hundred feet from the crossing. In the next four seconds, the fate of twenty-two men would be determined.

By the time Wolf's warning registered with Potter, the bus had traveled another twenty feet. The freshman looked to the right and saw the train rushing toward him. It was about sixty yards from the crossing. He momentarily took his foot off the accelerator and considered hitting the brakes. Then, judging that he wouldn't be able to stop the heavy bus on the slippery road soon enough, he stepped on the gas in an attempt to beat the train through the intersection. The situation's peril was immediately obvious to those on board. Slade jumped up and began struggling with the catch on the front door, facing the looming engine as he tried to escape. Some of the students at the back of the bus rose from their seats.

Near the Round Rock depot, a crowd gathered next to the destroyed Baylor bus alongside the tracks. Photograph courtesy of The Texas Collection, Baylor University.

With the engine almost upon them, Potter realized he wouldn't make it across the intersection in time and modified his initial plan. He desperately cut the wheels to the left and aimed for a point just east of the crossing, hoping the maneuver would secure enough ground to carry them over the tracks ahead of the engine. At the back of the bus, Weir Washam turned to the right and, partially carried by his forward momentum within the swerving bus, jumped toward the open window at his side. Abe Kelley scrambled behind his longtime friend for the same exit as he, too, attempted to escape.

Washam fell free and hit the ground on his chest. He drove his hands into the mud, coming to a stop only three feet from the tracks. The bus, having left the road, was making a jarring arc across the rails. Washam looked up just as the engine's cowcatcher rushed past. All but the rear section of the vehicle had cleared the tracks. He saw Kelley trying to get out through the open window. And then he saw the train collide with the bus at that exact spot.

—6—

AMONG THE DEAD

When the Sunshine Special's engine tore through the back of the bus, Abe Kelley and four others who had been sitting near him — Jack Castellaw, Sam Dillow, Bob Hailey, and Willis Murray — were killed by direct impact. Ivey Foster, sitting in the seat that Ed Gooch had charitably given him, was instantly killed by flying debris — the only one in the front two rows to die.

Up front, Louis Slade was thrown from the bus and landed in the mud, where he lay as the train passed by. The engine carried the bus a few yards, ripping the top and the back and right sides from the chassis, before sending it spinning off in a near circle on the south side of the tracks.

Dave Cheavens felt himself flying through the air and then realized that he was sprawled on the ground. He rose to his feet in the train's wake and confronted the nightmarish scene. Smashed wicker chairs and other pieces of wreckage were scattered for more than forty yards down the tracks. The bus was utterly demolished and empty of passengers. The team's green-and-gold jerseys lay in the mud alongside spare tires. He saw Dillow, Merle Dudley, William Winchester, and Bob Hannah lying motionless near one another.

Weir Washam ran over to Slade, and the two made their way toward Cheavens, who had started checking for signs of life. Coach Wolf, Keifer Strickland, and John Kane were also walking around, dazed and bleeding. The station agent from the Round Rock depot hurried over to them as the braking train hissed down the tracks. Cheavens picked up Hannah and helped carry him into the station, convinced the young man was dead. Coach Wolf directed the rescue efforts, showing remarkable presence of mind in the catastrophe's aftermath.

Washam's first thought was of Kelley. Unable to find his friend near the crash site, he began following the tracks toward the train, which had come to a stop about three hundred yards away. The Sunshine Special's crew streamed past Washam toward the wreckage, but he continued on until he came to the front of the engine. There, on the cowcatcher, hung the horribly mangled bodies of Kelley and Hailey. Another body, decapitated and crushed, lay caught in a nearby switch in the tracks.

As the able-bodied survivors carried the casualties into the station, several doctors and other Round Rock residents arrived at the scene. One woman, who lived a few blocks away, had pulled sheets from her clothesline to use as bandages. Hannah and Winchester were deemed the most gravely wounded of the survivors. The close friends were rushed off in a makeshift ambulance to Martin Hospital in nearby Georgetown.

Out on the tracks, the crew backed up the train to the depot while the recovery efforts continued. Two Baylor students hitchhiking to the game, Joe Holliday and Herman Caskey, had stopped at the crash site. With the help of a local newspaper reporter, they undertook the task of identifying the dead. The headless body at the switch was determined to be Jack Castellaw. A season's athletic pass issued to a woman—Castellaw's sweetheart, the Baylor students quickly noted—was found in one of his coat pockets.

With the coach's help, Cheavens used the team's scorebook to compile a list of passengers that indicated whether they had been killed or injured. He then placed a call to Baylor from the Missouri Pacific office to break the news. He also sent a telegram to the Associated Press. However, he failed to include his own name on the list of casualties, leading to an initial uncertainty about his fate as the afternoon papers around the state went to press with the story.

The twenty Baylor men remaining at the crash site—dead and wounded alike—were eventually put on board the Sunshine Special in the baggage car, beyond the train passengers' sight. A box containing body parts sat in a corner—a gruesome testimony to the impact's violence. In fact, switchmen and other depot employees would spend the rest of the cold day recovering remains amid blood-stained pools of rainwater. Finally, at 1:10 p.m., the train resumed its course, bound for Taylor fifteen miles to the northeast.

News of the catastrophe had reached Taylor well before the train pulled into the town forty-five minutes later. Doctors, nurses, and ambulance drivers formed part of the large, somewhat chaotic crowd on hand at the depot. When they entered the baggage car, they were shocked by what they saw. Several bodies lay in a corner. Wounded students were helping those with even worse injuries. A young man whose face was bleeding sat in the

Like other newspapers around the state, the Fort Worth Star-Telegram *devoted considerable space to news of the Round Rock tragedy on the front page of its January 23, 1927, edition. Photograph courtesy of The Texas Collection, Baylor University.*

middle of the car with one hand resting on a dead team-mate and the other stroking the head of an injured friend.

The doctors and nurses quickly began the process of transferring the injured men from the train to the Physicians and Surgeons Hospital and removing the life-less bodies for transportation to a funeral home. A local laundry owner was among the volunteers helping to carry out the dead students on stretchers. As the fourth body was being lifted, the blood-stained covering slipped off the victim's face. The businessman froze. It was his son, Ivey Foster Jr. He sank to his knees with a moan and was soon aided by nearby friends, who led him away from the horrible sight.

—7—

HEARTBREAKING NEWS

As the injured men began receiving medical treatment, Coach Wolf learned that William Winchester and Bob Hannah had died in the Georgetown hospital. Then came news that Merle Dudley and Jim Walker had died within minutes of reaching the hospital in Taylor. The fact that several of the remaining survivors, especially Fred Acree, were suffering from potentially fatal injuries added to the anguish.

Ed Gooch's brother, Tiny, the University of Texas football star, had traveled up from Austin with several teammates after hearing news of the accident, knowing that Ed had been on the bus. When he reached the hospital in Taylor, he gave a cry of joy upon discovering that his brother, though seriously wounded, was alive.

Washam's parents were at a hotel in Austin when they learned of the bus-train collision. In the lobby, a man who said he had spoken by telephone with someone in Georgetown told Washam's mother that her son had

been killed—perhaps confusing Weir Washam's name
with William Winchester's. Overwhelmed with grief, she
took solace in her husband's arms. However, just as the
Washams were preparing to leave for Taylor, a messen-
ger rushed up to them from the railroad office, where
information about the accident had been coming in, and
told them that not only had their son escaped death, but
his injuries were slight. Washam's mother promptly
kissed this bearer of good news.

Such moments of relief were rare on a day that, by
late afternoon, was marked by the confirmed deaths of
ten young men.

News of the tragedy in Round Rock quickly spread
across the state. In Lott, Bob Hailey's father was listen-
ing to the radio in anticipation of the broadcast of the
game against Texas. Then came an announcement about
the bus-train collision—with his son's name listed among
the dead.

Having left Waco immediately upon hearing about
the accident, Baylor's president, Samuel Palmer Brooks,
arrived in Taylor around four o'clock with football coach
and athletic director Morley Jennings and business manager George Belew. They divided the rest of the day
between trips to the Forwood Funeral Home, the hospital, and a hotel where some of the students' families had
already gathered.

Back in Waco, the residents of the Haunted House
heard about the fatal accident over the radio, though the
initial report lacked information about who had died.
Like many other Baylor students alerted to the tragedy,
they quickly made their way to various gathering places
around campus to learn the latest news—some waiting in

Samuel Palmer Brooks served as president of Baylor University from 1902 to 1931. Photograph courtesy of The Texas Collection, Baylor University.

the president's office, others at the Corner Drug Store. The names of the dead were solemnly circulated through the groups as soon as they were announced on the radio. The Haunted House men heard first that Abe Kelley had been killed. And then Jim Walker. And then their room-mate, Bob Hailey.

As Baylor students shared their grief with each other, trying to come to terms with the sudden loss of class-mates and friends, the school newspaper put out a special bulletin in the late afternoon. The first of what would become hundreds of telegrams of condolence soon began arriving at Baylor, sent by schools, civic groups, and individuals from across Texas and around the nation.

"The heart of Baylor University is torn to shreds at this moment," President Brooks told the press that day. "There will be no school classes at Baylor on Monday, of course, but there will be memorial exercises. But just now I can make no outline of what we shall do. We must be given time. Nothing like this has ever happened before."

After Dave Cheavens had his minor injuries dressed in a downtown Taylor office, he joined Louis Slade, Keifer Strickland, and Weir Washam, all of whom had been discharged from the hospital. The four men boarded a train at the Taylor depot and prepared for what would be a strange return home. During the trip, they sat in dazed silence, occasionally sharing a word or two about how awful things were.

An anxious crowd greeted the students when they arrived in Waco at six o'clock. Still in a state of shock and suffering from a blow to the head and a gashed cheek, Strickland was taken to a local hospital, where he would remain for several days. Meanwhile, Cheavens, Slade, and Washam made their way to the Baylor campus, where the press gathered to collect eyewitness accounts.

"I never saw anybody as good as Coach Wolf," Cheavens told a reporter from the *Dallas Morning News* from his bed in Brooks Hall. "He was carrying boys in and getting cushions and things for them from the time the train hit us almost. He did all he could for those boys."

In a sorrowful voice, Slade supplied details of the crash. "The train swept through the bus just as you would sweep through a room," he told reporters. "Had we just had time to think, many of the boys would have jumped. In the short time we had, though, we could not get the doors open, and those that escaped were simply luckily knocked out of the bus."

For his part, Washam sought some form of comfort at the fire department's Station No. 4, where he had spent many hours with Kelley. A *Waco Times-Herald* reporter accompanied Washam there and took notes for his story as the young man sat, broken-hearted, on Kelley's bed.

In St. Louis that night, Bob Hannah's father, Lee, boarded a train for Waco, where his wife, Mary Jane, had been staying the previous week. The couple's separation made their grief more keen. "Dear Lee, be brave," Mary Jane told him in a Western Union telegram that reached him en route. "We have each other. I am with you in spirit and wish I could be with you in person on this long, sad trip home."

The next day—Sunday, January 23—Ed Gooch woke up on his twenty-first birthday to find himself in a hospital bed. He had suffered a shoulder separation, broken ribs, and a gash on his neck. After learning why he was there, he was confronted by the knowledge that almost everyone who had been near him at the back of the bus was dead.

The Crash's Toll

Killed

Jack Castellaw

Sam Dillow

Merle Dudley

Ivey Foster Jr.

Robert Hailey
Robert Hannah Jr.
Clyde "Abe" Kelley
Willis Murray
James Walker
William Winchester

Seriously injured
Fred Acree Jr.
Wesley Bradshaw
Ed Gooch

Slightly injured
Gordon Barry
Cecil Bean
Dave Cheavens
John Kane
Joe Potter
Louis Slade
Keifer Strickland
Weir Washam
Ralph Wolf

—8—

DAYS OF MOURNING

Baylor officials took immediate steps to reach out to the families who had lost sons in the tragedy and to a close-knit campus community that included only ninety faculty members and a little more than fifteen hundred students. The university was a place where almost everyone knew each other, with students customarily greeting one another while passing from class to class.

Baylor was, moreover, an institution that Samuel Palmer Brooks had transformed during his twenty-five years as president, and now the university community needed his leadership to help guide it through this sudden calamity. The sixty-three-year-old Brooks had been a Baylor student himself, graduating in 1893 at the age of twenty-nine before going on to earn a master's degree from Yale University. His Baylor education had followed a childhood spent in poverty on his family's farm in Texas and a young adulthood spent working as a section hand on the Santa Fe Railroad and teaching school. Beloved by Baylor students, who called him "Prexy," he was an even-tempered man with a bald forehead, dark eyebrows, and a salt-and-pepper moustache. He was known as a man of character, compassion, and judiciousness who looked after Baylor students *in loco parentis* — a true father figure.

When he became president of Baylor, in 1902, Brooks assumed responsibility for a respected university that had been founded on the aspirations of Baptist pioneers and chartered in 1845 by the Republic of Texas. But in terms of academic standing, Baylor in 1902 was more of a small college with a regional reputation than a true university. The faculty consisted of twenty-nine members, with just five holding doctorates. And although the student body numbered approximately 750, only a third took college-level courses; the majority studied in Baylor's preparatory school. Having shaken off his "Texas provincialism" during his Ivy League years, as he once phrased it in a letter to his father, Brooks soon began implementing the "more advanced methods of teaching" he had experienced at Yale. He wanted Baylor to measure up to the best schools in the land.

After the 1903 addition of a College of Medicine, located in Dallas, Brooks focused his efforts on enhancing Baylor's strengths through institutional restructuring and strategic expansion, particularly during the years following World War I. From 1918 to 1921, he merged the departments of music and expression into a College of Fine Arts (later renamed the School of Music), placed the various areas of educational study within a School of Education, and brought together eighteen departments to form a College of Arts and Sciences. He also oversaw the establishment of a College of Dentistry in 1918 and the creation of a School of Law in 1920.

At the end of the 1925 school year, the editors of Baylor's yearbook, the *Round-Up*, printed an encomium toward the front of the book that, if perhaps overly heroic in its portraiture, conveyed the pride that Baylor students took in their longtime president:

> Samuel Palmer Brooks is recognized throughout the United States as one of the ablest administrators and educators of his day. An humble believer in the Almighty God, a man with a world vision, one who dares to do right, always a fearless soldier for the cause of justice, a clear thinker with a desirable sense of humor, he represents the highest type of American manhood and Christian democracy.

Leading Baylor through such an unprecedented tragedy—in the wake of the fatal halftime melee during the previous fall's football game against Texas A&M, no less—would require all the fortitude Brooks could muster. In a representative display of compassion, Brooks sent a telegram to Bob Hannah's parents the day after the collision. "I have just returned from Taylor whence I went yesterday noon for service to the dear boys," he wrote. "Baylor's heart is beside yours as you lay away the body of your son. May God comfort you."

As one of his first administrative acts following the accident, Brooks appointed ten groups, each composed of two faculty members and two students, to represent the university at the funeral services. They were quickly called into action. The funerals began on Sunday, when more than a thousand people attended the service for

Ivey Foster in Taylor. In the small town of Lott, churches suspended their services to allow the population to attend Bob Hailey's funeral at the Methodist church. The rain had continued falling overnight, making the streets too muddy for Hailey's body to be taken by hearse from the family's home. Consequently, the four pallbearers — all of whom were fellow football players and roommates at the Haunted House — carried the casket from the house to the church.

At ten o'clock on Monday, Baylor held a memorial service for the ten victims in the temporary chapel building. It was a damp, cold, and gray winter morning. The auditorium doubled as the basketball team's home court, and the goals' rims had been draped in green and gold for the occasion, with a streamer of black running through the school colors and a wreath of flowers placed atop each basket. The student body, faculty, Baylor board members, representatives of other institutions, and hundreds of people from Waco and across the state formed a crowd of more than three thousand. A large dark-green velvet curtain hung behind the platform. On one side of the speaker's rostrum stood a wreath of white flowers from Texas A&M, and on the other side was a basket of red carnations sent by SMU.

After an opening prayer, a quartet led the crowd in singing "My Faith Looks Up to Thee." President Brooks struggled to contain his grief when his turn came to speak. His voice broken with emotion and with tears flowing freely, he noted that only the "fellowship of suffering" made the tragedy bearable. "They were our boys — they can't know how much we loved them," he said before briefly talking about each of the ten dead students.

Among the service's other speakers was Henry Trantham, head of the athletic council. "Shall we then say with worldly wisdom that these young men were cut off in their prime, that their lives so full of promise were incomplete, that a blind fate has snatched them away?" he asked. "No, that were to yield the palm to death; that were to forget the blessed assurance that he who marks the sparrow's fall takes thought of his children. Their lives are lived, but not in vain. God's purpose is accomplished in them. The things they stood for are a part of the rich heritage of Baylor; their unconquerable spirit will hover around us in the years to come."

Also during that Monday morning, services were held in Abilene for Merle Dudley, in Fort Worth for Sam Dillow, and in Ennis for Jack Castellaw, who was

Willis Murray and James Walker were buried in adjacent plots in Gatesville's City Cemetery. Photograph courtesy of James Powell.

eulogized by well-known Baylor English professor A. J. Armstrong.

In the afternoon, a joint funeral service for Willis Murray and Jim Walker was held at the First Baptist Church of Gatesville, with an overflow crowd of hundreds. Rev. E. W. Bridges of the First Methodist Church led the service. Baylor professor T. H. Claypool spoke about the students, and Baylor professor W. P. Maroney delivered the sermon. Baylor was also represented by a group of students, six of whom acted as pallbearers. Afterward, the bodies of the two friends were conveyed to the city cemetery, where they were buried in adjacent plots later marked by matching headstones.

At three o'clock that afternoon, a crowd again filled Baylor's temporary chapel building, this time for a funeral service for the Waco trio of Abe Kelley, William Winchester, and Bob Hannah. A mayoral proclamation had called for all Waco businesses to close for the hour of the funeral, and the city's telephone service had been discontinued as well. Waco's schools had dismissed classes at two o'clock, every flag in the city flew at half-staff, and fire stations were draped in mourning in Kelley's honor.

Unable to find standing room within the auditorium, hundreds of people stood in silence outside in the bleak weather as the service began. Inside, a wealth of flowers banked the rostrum, at the foot of which rested three caskets. From the victims' families and close friends sitting up front to the people standing along the back wall, memories of the students and grief over their deaths united the crowd and deepened the poignancy of the successive prayers, hymns, and testimonials.

*Following the joint funeral service for Waco residents Robert Hannah Jr.,
Clyde "Abe" Kelley, and William Winchester in Baylor's temporary chapel
building, a crowd watched as pallbearers loaded the caskets into waiting
hearses. Photographs courtesy of The Texas Collection, Baylor University.*

Dean W. S. Allen spoke on behalf of the president, faculty, and students. "We do not understand, but our lives will be better for having known these boys," he said. "We loved them, and we cherish their memory. I have faith that God has a hand in everything. He watcheth over and comforteth the lives of those whom he called home—our boys."

The burials of Winchester and Hannah in Oakwood Cemetery and Kelley in the adjacent Park Lawn Cemetery marked the end of that day's sorrowful proceedings. The J. W. Speight Lodge, of which Kelley had been a member, performed Masonic rites at the athlete's grave. One of the pallbearers was Weir Washam—the image of his friend struggling to escape the bus just before the collision no doubt still fresh in his mind.

—9—

THE ACCIDENT'S AFTERMATH

While the funeral services were proceeding on Monday, January 24, a resolution offered by state legislator and Baylor graduate Robert Poage was passed by the Texas House of Representatives. In calling for the flag over the capitol to be lowered to half-staff for a day, the resolution described the accident's victims as being "worthy in every way to be acclaimed true sons of those great spirits who died at the Alamo and Goliad."

The next day, the headline for a story in the *Lariat* read, "Memorial Services Held for Immortal Ten." It was the first prominent use of the term, although Jack Hawkins, writing in the *Waco Times-Herald* on January 23, had used the poetic phrase in eulogizing the dead Baylor students: "Though Death's icy fingers have written 'Finis' across the life of each of the immortal ten who are today mourned, their memory will never perish."

Meanwhile, the crash's survivors, the victims' families and friends, and the university itself faced the prosaic reality of life in the tragedy's aftermath. On January 25, Baylor's athletic council canceled all remaining varsity and freshman basketball games. While some survivors soon returned to class, many remained under medical care. Dave Cheavens, unable to attend the memorial services, was confined to his dormitory bed for several days due to the accident's effect on his recovery from a recent appendicitis operation. Fred Acree was initially thought to have broken his back, his lower limbs being paralyzed until he moved a leg on the Sunday following the crash. After being moved to the Baptist Hospital in Waco in mid-February, he was placed in a plaster cast and hospitalized into March.

Former Baylor star Wesley Bradshaw's back was seriously injured in the accident, requiring surgery in mid-February, and he spent the next five months in and out of hospitals. There was a silver lining to his suffering, however. Later that year, he married the nurse, Nola Knight, whom he had met during his convalescence. Coach Wolf, who was treated for a three-inch-long scalp wound and several cuts to his face, came home to Waco four days after the accident to greet the latest addition to the Wolf family; his second child, Ralph, had been born during the time he was in the hospital at Taylor.

In the weeks following the loss of her son William, Katherine Winchester restricted her mourning to private moments as she tried to act as a pillar of strength for her husband and their two remaining sons—Albert and William's twin, Robert, both students at Baylor. Eventually, she began corresponding with another grieving parent—Mary Jane Hannah, Bob's mother. The two women had known each other, connected through their sons' friendship, prior to the Hannahs' move to St. Louis the previous spring.

"The longer it gets, the worse it seems to me," Mrs. Winchester wrote on March 10. "At first it seemed like the boys were just away and would soon return, but as time goes on it is almost unbearable. . . . I know I have two more smart boys, but my circle is broken and it hurts just as bad. I always go by Bob's grave, and it is real pretty. The pansies are blooming now. I went by myself one day and talked to Bob awhile and then William. It seems almost a sin to live when such sweet boys are gone."

Three weeks later, another letter from Mrs. Winchester traveled from Waco to St. Louis. "I dreamed William came in last night from hunting and I grabbed him and asked where he had been so long, and he said in his sweet, smiling way, 'Well, Mr. Hannah wanted to go to St. Louis,'" she wrote. "Then I waked up. . . . I try not to worry, but one third of my heart is buried and will always remain closed in sacred memory of my dear boy."

Keifer Strickland, who was close to the Hannah family, wrote several letters to his dead friend's mother. "I feel like you do lots of times, Mrs. Hannah, like I can't carry on—for it seems that this world and this life is just a false something, but there comes better days and I find consolation in others," he wrote on March 20. A month later, he was still feeling bereft: "Yes, I am tired of school. I have been ever since the accident. There has never been anything to take the heart out of me so much as that. I do hope I can find some sort of recompense." Seventeen years later, he would name his son Robert Hannah Strickland in honor of his late friend.

*Joe Potter, a freshman from West, was the driver of the athletic bus.
Photograph from the* Round-Up, Baylor University.

That hope for a compensatory discovery of meaning was common among those grieving the loss of friends and family members. Six weeks after their son's death, in a letter to President Brooks, Jack Castellaw's parents wrote, "We do know that if the going away of the ten dear boys including our own, our *all*, shall result in a greater Baylor; if the lives they touched shall be enriched; if the life of some boy or girl shall be made better, spurred on to nobler aims and higher ideals—then their sacrifice will not have been in vain."

Joe Potter, the freshman who had driven the bus into the catastrophe, was understandably burdened with a heavy heart in the following months. His Spanish professor, Andrés Sendón, was sympathetic to the young man's difficulty in resuming his studies. "I feel like sitting down and crying with him," Sendón confided to his wife. President Brooks, referring to Potter in a letter, said at the time, "The young man has been almost beside himself with grief and we are trying to build him up, for we know he did his best."

A few hours after the bus-train collision, Clarence E. Gilmore, chairman of the Texas Railroad Commission, issued a statement that referred to a similar, though less deadly, accident in 1926. "These constantly occurring accidents must demonstrate beyond controversy to every public official, to every railroad official and employee, and to every citizen the absolute necessity for concert of action both in matters of legislation and private endeavor to prevent these accidents," he said. Four days later, Missouri Pacific officials, having summoned the train's crew and several witnesses, convened a board of inquiry in Round Rock to investigate the circumstances of the crash.

Missouri Pacific's inquiry was but one of several pressing matters that required immediate attention in the aftermath of the tragedy. Legislation and litigation were two others.

On the day of the accident, Lee Bobbitt, speaker of the Texas House of Representatives, told the press that he would favor a law requiring railways to place automatic safety devices at all crossings. In addition, as the *Dallas Morning News* reported, "A bill requiring railroads and interurbans to build and maintain overhead or underground crossings at intersections with designated state and federal highways has been prepared for introduction in the House Monday by Representatives Roy Stout of Ennis and Roscoe Runge of Mason. The legislators drafted the bill shortly after learning of the tragedy at Round Rock."

The bill apparently failed to make headway in its initial version. On March 24, U.S. Senator Earle Mayfield of Texas wrote President Brooks to recommend that the university press have the state legislature, in a special session, pass a statute providing for overpasses or underpasses to be built at railroad grade crossings. "The separation of railroad crossings at grade, in Texas, is a stupendous undertaking," the senator wrote. "It cannot be accomplished in a year or even in five years, but it will take a long time to bring about the separation of all of the dangerous railroad grade crossings in our state. However, when this great work has been accomplished, it will solve absolutely one of the most serious problems now confronting the people of Texas." Mayfield closed his letter by stating that he would gladly join Brooks in encouraging Texas Governor Dan Moody to pursue the initiative.

Political circumstances, however, would complicate the matter, as Brooks predicted in his response to the senator on March 29. "I certainly would be happy if something like you suggest could be carried out," he wrote. "I doubt materially if Mr. Moody would call a special session or make a special recommendation for this matter at this time, particularly as it was not a part of his platform demands. If I am correctly informed through the press, he is seeking to carry out his platform first before entering upon new enterprises."

The Texas Highway Department eventually implemented a program of eliminating grade crossings, typically by relocating highways, but eight years would pass before an overpass was constructed across the tracks in Round Rock.

The process of victims' families and survivors filing lawsuits against the International-Great Northern Railroad Company proceeded at a quicker pace. Writing to Mary Jane Hannah on March 31, Katherine Winchester provided an update on her family's legal situation. "I saw the office girl of our lawyer, and she said he thought it wise to wait and see what the others were doing before filing suit as he said the case would not come up any sooner by filing now," she wrote. "The railroad has made Baylor co-defendants, the paper stated. The girl told me not to say anything about what she told me, but I tell you and of course you won't tell it. They think it wise to keep silence as much as possible."

Wesley Bradshaw was one of the first survivors to seek damages for his injuries, initially filing suit against the railroad company for negligence. As Mrs. Winchester had learned, the railroad company, in turn, sued Baylor, seeking indemnity from or a shared responsibility for any damages. But after Bradshaw's suit resulted in a mistrial, the railroad company paid Bradshaw $6,500 in November 1927 in exchange for his agreement not to pursue further action against it.

Bradshaw subsequently sued Baylor and the insurance company that held a $50,000 policy on the school's bus. However, the Bradshaw-Baylor suit's resolution would take several years and a ruling by the Supreme Court of Texas to be reached.

Baylor's response to Bradshaw's suit was to sue International-Great Northern and to assert that the

railroad company's agreement with Bradshaw consti-
tuted a settlement of the matter. The jury disagreed, and
the district court rendered judgment in favor of
Bradshaw for $6,500, although it additionally ruled in
favor of Baylor's plea against the railroad company for
half of the damages. Baylor and the railroad company
appealed the decision to the Court of Civil Appeals,
which in 1932 reversed the lower court's ruling by decid-
ing that Bradshaw should receive no damages from
Baylor and that, by extension, the university should
receive no funds from the railroad company.

It was then Bradshaw's turn to appeal, and the
Supreme Court of Texas agreed to hear the case. In what
would become a frequently cited decision, on July 17,
1935, the Texas Supreme Court affirmed the Court of
Civil Appeals's judgment in the following ruling: "One
who was injured in a collision between a motor bus and
railroad train and who contracted with the railroad company for a stipulated sum on condition that he would not
sue the company, but would transfer to it whatever right
of suit he might have against the owner of the motor bus
with authority to sue in his name, is not entitled to further claims for damages." In short, the railroad company's $6,500 settlement with Bradshaw was all he
would receive for his pains.

Baylor's legal matters occupied President Brooks
and the university's representatives on several fronts
and—as proved to be the case with the Bradshaw suit—
for several years. It was, no doubt, a draining experience
for all involved.

On November 19, 1930, Brooks wrote to a corre-
spondent after spending the previous day in court in

Georgetown. "The abominable thing about the Georgetown matter is that the I. & G. N. railroad is suing Baylor
University in essence for the amount of money which the
railroad paid as damages to several families for the
deaths of their boys several years ago in the Round Rock
accident," he wrote. "They do not expect to get a penny
out of the university, but in this way hope to force the
university to cover the possible success of the case by the
indemnity bond—all of which is very technical and
nobody knows what will be done, except the general feeling that nothing can fall upon the university."

When Brooks sat down to write this letter in late
1930, he had more than just the lingering consequences
of the Round Rock tragedy on his mind, for he was facing additional challenges that, in their totality, were
daunting. For the previous two months, he had been
busily engaged in Baylor's campaign to raise $500,000 to
pay off the university's debts. He was also under a physical burden. The previous summer, during a tour of
Europe, he had injured himself while trying to move
some baggage and had been operated on in September to
remedy the problem. His health, however, had not fully
returned. He was losing weight. As exploratory surgery
would reveal in the spring, he was suffering from abdominal cancer that would prove fatal.

—10—

AN UNDYING SPIRIT

In covering the Round Rock tragedy, the press quickly focused on a remarkable vignette within the overall story—the episode of Abe Kelley pushing Weir Washam to safety in the moments before the crash. Several of the surviving passengers, in giving their eyewitness accounts to reporters, noted that Washam had jumped through the open window at his side. But a few of them additionally said that Kelley had helped him escape.

"Weir Washam, the fifth boy on the back seat, jumped a second before the train hit," Louis Slade told a *Waco Times-Herald* reporter. "Kelley was right behind him and was ready to spring just as the locomotive ploughed into us."

Dave Cheavens described a more complex sequence of events, telling the press, "Abe Kelley shouted to Weir Washam, who was on the back seat, to jump out the window, and he helped Weir out."

But John Kane's version of the action at the back of the bus was even more dramatic. A story titled "Kelley

Sacrificed Life to Save His Fellow Teammate" that ran on the front page of the *Dallas Morning News* the day after the accident summarized his account: "Kane said Kelley deliberately pushed Washam out of a rear window of the bus when the train was seen bearing down on the bus, and the diminutive Baylor athlete was thus saved. Kelley could have jumped himself, but he preferred to give the open window to his friend, whom he pushed through the window."

In providing his own narrative of the crash to reporters, Washam never mentioned receiving assistance from Kelley. In later years, during private conversations, he would deny that Kelley had pushed him, although he never publicly refuted the claim out of respect for his longtime friend.

In the end, Kane's account, which was reported by the major newspapers across the state, provided the basis for what would become the widely accepted story of Abe Kelley's heroism. During a radio address on February 1, 1927, President Brooks endorsed Kane's portrait of Kelley's last act. "The awful event has given the world a glowing example of unselfishness, wherein Abe Kelley, who could have saved his own life, instead pushed out of the window his friend, Weir Washam," Brooks said. "Kelley went to his death. Washam was unhurt. While the memory of men remains sound in Texas, this heroic deed will be cherished."

The true nature of Kelley's role in Washam's escape will never be known for certain—whether he played absolutely no part in it, on one extreme; whether he displayed split-second heroism, on the other extreme; or whether he simply found his own passage to survival blocked by his friend and, out of necessity, gave him a push that Washam didn't feel in the chaos of the moment.

The story of Abe Kelley can be considered a microcosm of the larger story of the fatal accident, for dissimilar versions of what happened on January 22, 1927, soon took shape.

In one version, ten brave students had died fighting for Baylor, not unlike soldiers on a battlefield. As the Texas House of Representatives had stated in its resolution, the crash's victims were "worthy in every way to be acclaimed true sons of those great spirits who died at the Alamo and Goliad."

This was a frequent public characterization of the dead students in the immediate wake of the accident. "This morning a pathetic, tragic scene was unfolded at the Katy station," Jack Hawkins wrote in the *Waco Times-Herald* on January 23. "Puffing into the station through the fogs of early morning, and looming through the mists like a ghostly cortege, arrived a train bearing the bodies of five of those who were killed. A solemn, sorrowing, reverent crowd was waiting. Loving hands tenderly lifted the hallowed remains of those stalwart heroes—for heroes they were, each one." And on February 6, *Waco News-Tribune* sports editor Jinx Tucker wrote of the accident, "When the startling news was broadcast by every conceivable modern means of how death riding with a speeding express had taken from the very threshold of life ten Texans, who in death's relentless grasp typified all of the valor, fortitude, and courage for which their forefathers won everlasting glory, the state of Texas first recoiled in horror at the shock."

Though such portrayals of the students contained inaccuracies and exaggerations, they possessed a psychological utility, consoling the bereaved through the lofty language of eulogy. But for many of the passengers who survived the crash, the memory of that awful day formed a second, private version of the Round Rock tragedy. Theirs was a story full of ambiguities, unanswered questions, and painfully remembered details that had little in common with the story of sacrifice, bravery, and heroism that the community embraced. And, by and large, theirs was a story never put into words. It was a story they simply carried with them as they went on to earn Baylor degrees before spreading out across the map to establish careers and families with their spared lives.

Many of the survivors pursued careers in coaching and education, helping to shape numerous young men and women. After serving as captain and earning all-conference honors as a forward on Baylor's 1928 basketball team, Keifer Strickland had a lengthy teaching career at Sunset High School in Dallas, where he also coached baseball for several years, before his death in 1992. Gordon Barry was a school superintendent in the Hondo Independent School District and lived to be eighty-seven. Wesley Bradshaw held coaching and teaching positions at several colleges and high schools in Texas and Arkansas, including a turn as Ouachita Baptist College's head football coach, before dying in 1960 while visiting relatives in his hometown of Athens. And Cecil Bean ended his career in education as the principal of Irvin High School in El Paso, where he died in 1976.

The careers of the other survivors varied considerably, as one might expect.

Fred Acree worked as a scientist for thirty-nine years in the U.S. Department of Agriculture—at one point co-authoring a scientific paper, titled "Synthesis of 8-Isoamyl-7-Methoxcoumarin," that was published in the *Journal of the American Chemical Society*. He died in 2001 at the age of ninety-three.

After playing as the starting center of the varsity basketball team during his senior year and graduating from Baylor in 1928, Louis Slade became a widely respected saddle-maker. Though he practiced his trade at some of the nation's top saddle producers—with stops at Hamley and Company in Pendleton, Oregon, and N. Porter Saddle and Harness Company in Phoenix, Arizona—he spent the majority of his years working in Uvalde at the Slade Saddle Shop, which his father established in 1929. He died on January 22, 1980—exactly fifty-three years after the crash in Round Rock.

Weir Washam, who had so dramatically escaped sure death, played two more years as the football team's star quarterback. During his final season, in 1928, he had a fifty-yard, touchdown-scoring run in the game against Rice, which the school yearbook described as "a fitting climax for the smallest, gamest, and one of the most feared men in the conference." After earning a degree in business administration and economics in 1929, he coached Baylor's freshman football and basketball teams for a year before going on to coach football and teach at high schools in Tahoka and Alice. A career change brought him into the employment of Brown and Root

Construction Company, for which he held a variety of positions that included the company's agent for the paving of city streets throughout West Texas. He died in Midland at the age of fifty-one.

The team's coach, Ralph Wolf, remained at Baylor until 1954, coaching the 1932 team to Baylor's first SWC championship in basketball. During his long Baylor career, he was also the director of athletics and, ultimately, the executive vice president and general manager of the Baylor Stadium Corporation that oversaw the construction of a new football stadium. In addition, he maintained a simultaneous career in public service, being elected mayor of Waco in 1952. He was serving in that capacity when a powerful tornado struck Waco on May 11, 1953, and destroyed much of the downtown business district while claiming 114 lives. Wolf handled this second tragedy of his career with the same grace and skill he had shown in 1927. "Ralph Wolf took his rightful place at the head of disaster work with extra energy and zeal from his own rugged personality," the *Waco News-Tribune* wrote in an editorial. "It was a most fortunate meeting of man and destiny." A month after the tornado, the city held "Ralph Wolf Night," during which Texas Governor Allan Shivers stated, "For every great tragedy that arises to test humanity, a great leader is born. You've got yours here in Waco—in Ralph Wolf." Wolf left Waco in 1954 to become city manager of Orange and, a year later, executive director of the Texas Building Commission. He died in 1971.

John Kane—the young man considered a prime physical specimen by his teammates, though he never earned a starter's role—achieved renown as a B-24 bomber commander during World War II. He received the Medal of Honor for his role in "Operation Tidal Wave," a large-scale bombing raid on the Nazis' heavily guarded complex of oil refineries in Ploesti, Romania. Col. Kane visited Baylor in 1945 for a speech on the new United Nations before being assigned to the National War College in Washington, D.C. He died in 1996 at the age of eighty-nine and was buried in Arlington National Cemetery in Arlington, Virginia.

Several survivors maintained close ties with their alma mater. Joe Potter and Ed Gooch did so through their membership in the Baylor Chamber of Commerce. Potter regularly returned to Baylor for Homecoming, where he would fondly reminisce with fellow Chamber alumni about their college days. Understandably, he avoided talking about what had happened in Round Rock. In his later years, spent in retirement in Moody after having worked as an oil company safety supervisor, he rebuffed writers' attempts to interview him regarding the tragedy. He had gone on to achieve acclaim as a football and baseball player during his time at Baylor, and he was tired, he told such visitors, of being known only as the person who had driven the bus. He lived until 1994.

Gooch was similarly disinclined to talk about the crash. Though he would acknowledge that the accident had been a defining moment for him, he was the kind of person who focused on the positive things in life. And there had been plenty of positives; he and his wife, "Nip," had a long marriage with two children in the East Texas town of Gilmer, where he owned and operated a lumber and building materials store named Construction Supply

Ed Gooch, a survivor of the crash, looked at clippings about the accident during a visit to Baylor in 1980. Photograph by Mike James, courtesy of The Texas Collection, Baylor University.

Company, and he was honored in 1981 as Outstanding Citizen of Upshur County. However, in 1980 the organizers of the annual Freshman Mass Meeting, at which the story of the Immortal Ten is told, convinced him to tape a message to be played at the event. "When you have a close encounter, it makes you realize how really wonderful life is," he said. "I challenge each of you every morning as you wake to thank God for the day before you and to think of the many good things that will happen to you this day. Dwell on the good, then you can better accept the bad and the disappointments and overcome any obstacles." He died on Christmas in 1990, just a few weeks after he and his wife had celebrated their sixtieth wedding anniversary.

Of the survivors, Dave Cheavens spoke the most frequently and openly about the crash. After becoming chairman of Baylor's journalism department in the early 1960s, following an accomplished career as a journalist, he was asked to share his story with Baylor students in a Chapel program in 1964. "It was one of these things that happens without rhyme or reason. But there was something here that kept the tragedy from becoming destructive," he said, before describing how Kelley had helped save Washam's life. "To me this example holds the refined essence of this intangible thing that those of us who know and love Baylor call the Baylor spirit." He told the same story in later years, although remembering the tragedy remained painful. After one such presentation, he told Baylor's chaplain, WJ Wimpee, that it would be his last. "That is so heart-wrenching," he said. "I just don't want to be asked to do that anymore."

A few years later, Cheavens wrote a letter to Janie Castellaw after she had given Baylor funds to build the Castellaw Communications Center in honor of her son, Jack. "I, too, was a passenger in that bus, but the Lord spared my life," Cheavens told her. "From that day to this, I have felt an obligation and challenge to dedicate my talents in writing for the good of mankind." On December 8, 1970, Cheavens died in Bryan, where he was attending a journalism conference. He was sixty-three years old. Only two months earlier, a *Lariat* reporter had asked him to compare the Round Rock tragedy to a recent plane crash in which members of Wichita State's football team had died. "Baylor was a very small school at that time. Everybody knew personally the athletes who were killed," he said. "It left the campus paralyzed. The emotional impact of something like that—you just can't recover from it. You remember sitting in class with those fellows, and the next week you go to class and they aren't there. It's quite a feeling."

Several decades after the cold, wet day on which Baylor's athletic bus approached a set of train tracks in Round Rock, that sense of absence is renewed every time the Immortal Ten are honored at the annual Freshman Mass Meeting. But in a way, those ten students are still in class at Baylor University, their ambitions, talents, and personalities reflected in those of today's students. After all, there is a kinship between students, based on certain unchanging aspects of the college experience, that crosses the boundaries of time. And the spirit of the Immortal Ten, handed down from generation to generation, is revived each fall as freshmen hear a part of the tale and take it along with them through the length of their days.

Such a cross-generational enterprise was at the heart of the last statement that Baylor President Samuel Palmer Brooks made. After exploratory surgery had revealed advanced abdominal cancer in early May of 1931, his doctors gave him two weeks to live. As the days passed, he realized that he wouldn't be able to deliver his customary message to the graduating class. Thus, on his deathbed, he took pen in hand and wrote what would later be called "The Immortal Message"—a title aptly echoing the epithet given to the ten students whose deaths he had so deeply mourned. Brooks died on May 14, with obituaries following in *The New York Times*, *Time* magazine, and other publications across the state and nation. His written remarks were read to the graduating class by acting president W. S. Allen:

This, my message to the Senior Class of 1931, I address also to the seniors of all years, those seniors of the past and those seniors yet to be. This I do because I love them all equally even as I love all mankind regardless of station or creed, race, or religion.

I stand on the border of mortal life, but I face eternal life. I look backward to the years of the past to see all pettiness, all triviality shrink into nothing and disappear. Adverse criticism has no meaning now. Only the worthwhile things, the constructive things, the things that have built for the good of mankind and the glory of God count now. There is beauty, there is joy, and there is laughter in life—as there ought to be. But remember, all of you, not to regard lightly nor to ridicule the sacred things, those worthwhile things. Hold them dear, cherish them, for they alone will sustain you in the end; and remember too that only through work and ofttimes through hardships may they be attained. But the compensation of blessing and sweetness at the last will glorify every hour of work and every heartache from hardship.

Looking back now as I do, I see things with a better perspective than ever before and in their truer proportions. More clearly do I recognize that God is love. More clearly do I understand the universal fatherhood of God. More clearly do I know the brotherhood of man.

Truths do not change. The truths of life which I learned as a student at Baylor have not varied, nor will they vary. I know now that life has been a summary of that which was taught me first as a student here. As my teachers have lived through me so I must live through you, my students. You who are graduating today will go out into the world to discover that already you have touched much of what the future holds. You have learned the lessons which must fit you for the difficulties and the joys of the years to come. Then hold these college years close in your hearts and value them at their true worth.

Do not face the future with timidity nor with fear. Face it boldly, courageously, joyously. Have faith in what it holds. Sorrow as well as happiness must come with time. But know that only after sorrow's hand has bowed your head will life become truly real to you, for only then will you acquire the noble spirituality which intensifies the reality of life. My own faith as I approach eternity grows stronger day by day. The faith I have had in life is projected into the vast future toward which I travel now. I know that I go to an all-powerful God wherever he may be. I know that he is a personality who created man in his image. Beyond that I have no knowledge—no fear—only faith.

Because of what Baylor has meant to you in the past, because of what she will mean to you in the future, oh my students, have a care for her. Build upon the foundations here the great school of which I have dreamed, so that she may touch and mold the lives of future generations and help to fit them for life here and hereafter. To you seniors of the past, of the present, of the future I entrust the care of Baylor University. To you I hand the torch.

My love be unto you and my blessing be upon you.

Appendix 1

A TRADITION OF REMEMBRANCE

"The names of ten boys have been taken from the roll of earth and registered in heaven," English professor A. J. Armstrong wrote in the January 25, 1927, edition of the *Daily Lariat*, Baylor's student newspaper. "Today every student knows the names of his fellow students who on Saturday were almost instantly hurled into Eternity. Today those names are written in gold across the pages of Baylor history and today those names are enshrined in love and reverence in the hearts of sixteen hundred Baylor students."

Today, several decades later, Baylor students still reverently remember the names of those ten students who died in the bus-train collision at Round Rock. From Jack Castellaw to William Winchester, the Immortal Ten are alphabetically presented as their story is told at the annual Freshman Mass Meeting, held on the Wednesday night of Baylor University's Homecoming week. They have become a hallowed tradition, symbolizing the unify-

*The Freshman Mass Meeting concludes with a candle-lighting ceremony
that celebrates the Baylor spirit represented by the Immortal Ten.
Photograph courtesy of Baylor Photography, Baylor University.*

ing Baylor spirit celebrated in the concluding candle-
lighting ceremony that takes place outside in the late-
night darkness of autumn.

The event's solemnity and origin in a matter of distant history might give today's freshmen the impression
that they are participating in a ritual that has remained
unchanged over the years. It is a tradition, after all, and
a tradition implies immutability. But the roll call of the
long absent has a long history of its own, one punctuated
by lapses in observance and characterized by several plot
twists.

In a way, this tradition began with a set of scrapbooks. In the months following the tragedy in Round
Rock, Elizabeth "Bess" Autrey Jennings, the wife of

football coach and athletic director Morley Jennings, produced three large scrapbooks concerning the students who were killed. Bound by the Baylor University Press in black boards with "The Immortal Ten" imprinted in gilt lettering on each cover, the scrapbooks bear the signature of careful preservation and respectful commemoration that would come to typify the story as told by succeeding generations.

In the first volume, Bess Jennings pasted clipped news accounts of the accident and biographical materials on the scrapbook's pages. The second and third volumes contain hundreds of telegrams and letters of condolence sent to Baylor by institutions, groups, and individuals from across the nation. "When you have viewed these three volumes, I believe you will be, as I have been, drawn closer to the 'Immortal Ten,'" Jennings wrote on April 23, 1927, as an inscription. "Sorrow has been routed by joy in doing every hour of this work. The purpose of the compiler will have been accomplished if you, as the reader, are brought closer to the men who have such a dear, deep spot in all our hearts."

During the regular Chapel period on Monday, January 23, 1928—the school day closest to the first anniversary of the tragedy—a memorial service was held for the Immortal Ten. Floral offerings for the graves of Wacoans Clyde "Abe" Kelley, William Winchester, and Robert Hannah Jr. adorned the stage, and a collection was taken to purchase floral arrangements for the homes of the seven other victims' families. The service included four brief speeches—two by students and two by faculty members. "Then we were suffering the agony of an awful wound, newly made," said Dr. E. N. Jones, contrasting the event with the previous year's memorial service. "Now, as our president has suggested, we meet in a spirit of triumphal memory." The journalism library, containing a bookcase specially designed to hold Bess Jennings's three scrapbooks, was kept open for the day to allow students and guests the opportunity to stop by and remember the dead. The mothers of Hannah and Winchester were among the visitors.

For the next three years, Baylor held a similar memorial service in Chapel on or near the anniversary of the bus-train collision. But the practice seems to have ended after President Samuel Palmer Brooks's death, in 1931. In 1934, the *Lariat* began printing a tribute to the Immortal Ten in observation of the anniversary date. For three years, the tribute ran on the first page of the newspaper, but in 1937 it drifted back to the second page, where it remained through 1939. And then, on the crash's anniversary in 1940, the Immortal Ten went unmentioned. With that, January 22 had effectively ceased to be a date of special observation on the Baylor calendar.

Enter the Freshman Mass Meeting, held in the fall of each year to begin Homecoming activities. Described as having begun in 1928 in honor of the Round Rock victims, the event was created to promote school spirit among freshman men by reviewing Baylor traditions and ideals. However, historical sources are inconclusive as to whether the specific tradition of the Immortal Ten was consistently observed during the event's initial years of existence. Pat Groner, a 1941 Baylor graduate, remembered the students' story being told each year, during the late 1930s and early 1940s, as part of the program. Then came the United States' entry into World War II—and with it the suspension of Homecoming the following fall. In 1946 the Freshman Mass Meeting and all other Homecoming activities resumed. But according to former Baylor professor Frank Leavell, who was a freshman that year, "The Immortal Ten was not the subject" of the meeting. Instead, the event consisted of testimonials about the greatness of Baylor.

However, in 1947 the story of the Immortal Ten entered a golden era of prominence and innovative presentation. That year the Freshman Mass Meeting, held on Thursday night, October 30, in Rena Marrs McLean Gymnasium, was "conducted by the yell leaders and dedicated to the Immortal Ten," the *Lariat* reported. The next morning, the story was told in Waco Hall during Chapel—primarily for the benefit of Baylor's female students, who remained excluded from the Mass Meeting. The Chapel presentation was staged as a live radio dramatization, transmitted from Baylor's radio studio. Edgar Will, an instructor in the radio department, wrote the script, and speech student Eddie Fadal produced and directed the performance. Two men narrated the story, accompanied by a cast of seniors playing the parts of the Immortal Ten. Sound effects and background organ music added to the presentation's drama.

During the next two decades, the one-two combination of the Freshman Mass Meeting and a Chapel presentation continued to keep the story alive. For a time, the senior class took charge of presenting the Chapel program. In 1964, crash survivor Dave Cheavens, then chairman of Baylor's journalism department, shared his memories with students attending Chapel. But soon afterward, the Freshman Mass Meeting became the tradition's sole home, with the creation in 1967 of a separate Women's Mass Meeting, held the night before the men's gathering, making a Chapel program on the Immortal Ten redundant. In 1972, the two meetings were merged.

The organizers of the Freshman Mass Meeting made a few more changes to the ceremony in following years — most significantly, the elimination of the spirit flame, sometimes called the eternal torch. For two decades, upperclassmen had presented the freshman class with a flame representing the Baylor spirit. In 1953, the flame came in the form of a candle, which was then used to light a torch that freshmen were required to keep burning until it, in turn, was used to ignite the Homecoming bonfire on Friday night. In 1955, a torch was simply

A traditional part of the annual Freshman Mass Meeting is representing the ten students who died in the 1927 bus-train crash. This photograph was taken during the late 1960s at one of the women's separate mass meetings in Rena Marrs McLean Gymnasium. Photograph courtesy of The Texas Collection, Baylor University.

handed over to streamline the process. This ceremony took another turn in 1964 when, after the passing of the torch, the men lit candles from the flame to complete the program.

In 1974, the Freshman Mass Meeting's format and location underwent significant changes to remedy a few problematic matters. First, the gathering was moved from Marrs McLean Gymnasium to the hillside at the Baylor Marina after complaints that spilled kerosene from the torch and wax drippings from hundreds of lit candles had damaged the gym's polished floor and grandstands. Second, the spirit flame was extinguished to eliminate the sophomore class's vigorous efforts to steal the torch from freshmen. "In the past few years, it's gotten to the point that everyone comes just to see the fight at the end over the Spirit Flame," Kent Reynolds, that year's Homecoming committee chairman for the Baylor Chamber of Commerce, said at the time. "It won't even be presented so that people will come with the intention of thinking on Homecomings of the past."

The format change effectively returned the focus of the annual gathering to the Immortal Ten, with the continuation of the concluding candle-lighting ceremony now more directly connected to the unifying Baylor spirit represented by the students. The spirit flame was eventually brought back—along with the sophomore class's high jinks—and a few more changes were implemented in following years, such as the establishment of ten o'clock as the event's starting hour and its relocation to Waco Hall in the 1990s.

Since 1985, Neil Knighton, a 1975 Baylor graduate, has been the person who tells the story of the Immortal

Ten at the event. As a student, he was a member of the Baylor Chamber of Commerce, and he felt the group's close connection to what happened in Round Rock in 1927. Two of those who died were Chamber members, and another had been elected to join the organization the week before the accident. As a result of those bonds and the organization's role as a tradition-oriented group, the Chamber of Commerce became the guardian of the Immortal Ten story by staging the Freshman Mass Meeting. In the 1980s, its members occasionally left flowers at the crash site on the tragedy's anniversary and once collected railroad spikes from the tracks, which were passed down to pledges.

Perhaps it is natural that members of Chamber, steeped in Baylor's traditions, would feel the power of the Immortal Ten. But what significance do other Baylor students find in such an old story?

"One of the issues I try to bring out in my closing is that we don't make heroes out of these young men," Knighton said, describing his presentation. "They are your roommates, or the friend across the hall, or the quiet guy that's a good athlete who maybe isn't the most popular guy on campus. These were kids just like the ones you're sitting next to tonight. The hero is the spirit of the Baylor tradition, and what we celebrate is acknowledging one another as important. Tradition is bound up in our relationships that we carry on for a lifetime. The stories help us enhance those relationships. That is the Baylor tradition."

Appendix 2

A PROPER MEMORIAL

"I am standing in a little pent-up room, talking into the microphone, a disk apparently useless, made with human hands. It strains my credulity to think that through it you hear my voice," Baylor President Samuel Palmer Brooks said when he took to the airwaves on February 1, 1927, to deliver an address to alumni from radio station WJAD. Radio was still in its early years, but Brooks's strained credulity was more showmanship than genuine skepticism. He recognized the medium's power, and he was counting on his voice being heard.

The occasion was the annual Founders' Day program, celebrating the eighty-second anniversary of Baylor's founding. After a few standard entreaties about the university's endowment needs, Brooks moved into an account of how Baylor was coping with the Round Rock tragedy, which had occurred only ten days earlier. His words of comfort, and his endorsement of a suggestion to build a memorial to the ten dead students, made it clear that the president knew his message had an audience of thousands of potential donors.

"There are those who think that Texas, all Texas, would like to get together and erect a memorial building on the Baylor campus in honor of our ten immortals," he said into the microphone. "Should this be done, it should be by all Texas, not merely by Baylor people. The suggestion gives opportunity to every unselfish nature in all the commonwealth to perpetuate the names of these boys. A half-million-dollar auditorium with a suitable marble column for each boy would be worthy. It cannot be done by Baylor alone, but benevolent people united can do it."

Brooks wasn't necessarily attempting to capitalize on the tragedy. True, the school needed a more suitable facility for daily Chapel than the temporary, barn-like building, which doubled as a gymnasium, that had been built after the Carroll Chapel and Library's destruction by fire in 1922. That need likely made the idea for an auditorium stand out from the many suggestions for memorials that had recently crossed the president's desk.

On February 6, *Waco News-Tribune* sports editor Jinx Tucker promoted the memorial auditorium proposal in a lengthy column. "The structure would be so built that its grandeur would put to shame other buildings on the campus," Tucker wrote. "While the courageous sons of Texas it is honoring are living in a happier land where they will never die, this memorial will not only tell its story of love, of a state torn with anguish, to the present generation, but when those who have built it have passed on, the same white columns in their stately grandeur will unfold a tale of tragedy, devotion, and love that will cause those of another generation to marvel and wonder as they listen with awe and reverence."

Brooks's radio address and Tucker's column generated considerable interest. Politicians, presidents of other universities, and newspaper editorialists expressed support for the proposal in the following days. And some donations, though modest, began coming in. The *Waco Farm and Labor Journal*, for example, sent ten dollars to Brooks. But in a March 29, 1927, letter to U.S. Senator Earle Mayfield of Texas, Brooks wrote of the proposed auditorium, "I fear that the idea has not struck sufficiently deep in the hearts of the people for a suitable memorial to be erected. Of this now I am not at all sure, because the young men who are working at it have not yet given up hopes, but I am speaking candidly of what appears to me to be a fact."

As time went on, the lack of funds necessary to build a large-scale memorial became a certainty. A less ambitious plan was to plant trees on the first anniversary of the tragedy. Money for the project was collected in the spring of 1927, but this initiative was soon abandoned because any of the possible sites for the trees could have been superseded by a planned women's dormitory whose location had yet to be determined. In the end, any lingering hope for a memorial auditorium was complicated and eventually dashed by developments stemming from an April 1928 recommendation made by the Education Commission of the Baptist General Convention of Texas (BGCT). At the time, the BGCT appointed the entirety of the school's Board of Trustees. The commission's recommendation was that Baylor—located in Waco since 1886—relocate to Dallas, which had pledged $1.5 million and a large piece of land as incentives for the move. For a time, the university's uncertain future in Waco effectively tabled the memorial auditorium proposal. And when alumni and the citizens of Waco, responding to the challenge from Dallas, began contributing funds to build a stately auditorium for the university as evidence of the city's ability to help Baylor prosper, the memory of the Immortal Ten didn't factor into the plans. Waco eventually won the day, and Baylor stayed put. When Waco Hall was dedicated on May 27, 1930, the structure stood devoid of any stately columns unfolding a tale of tragedy, devotion, and love.

As a result of those proposals' abandonment, for decades the only campus memorial to the Immortal Ten would be a bronze plaque that the men of S. P. Brooks Hall paid for and placed outside the dormitory's club room in 1927. Three of the victims—Ivey Foster Jr., Willis Murray, and James Walker—were living in Brooks Hall at the time of their deaths, and three others had previously lived there. "In memory of our comrades who died for Baylor in the Round Rock tragedy," reads the plaque, now located in The Texas Collection at Baylor.

Eight years after the bus-train collision, a bridge was built across the tracks in Round Rock. The overpass was the result of a drawn-out legislative effort, begun immediately after the tragedy, to eliminate railroad grade crossings by requiring the construction of overpasses or underpasses for highways. The bridge's dedication on February 12, 1935, was the occasion for the unveiling of a square plaque on which a brief statement and the ten victims' names were embossed.

DEDICATED BY THE STATE HIGHWAY
COMMISSION OF TEXAS TO THE MEMORY
OF THE MEMBERS OF AN ATHLETIC
TEAM OF BAYLOR UNIVERSITY WHO LOST
THEIR LIVES IN AN ACCIDENT AT THIS
CROSSING ON JANUARY TWENTY-SECOND
NINETEEN HUNDRED AND TWENTY-SEVEN.

JACK CASTELLAW	ENNIS
SAM DILLOW	FT. WORTH
MERLE H. DUDLEY	ABILENE
IVEY R. FOSTER, JR.	TAYLOR
ROBERT R. HAILEY	LOTT
ROBERT L. HANNAH, JR.	WACO
JAMES CLYDE KELLY	WACO
WILLIS EDWIN MURRAY	GATESVILLE
JAMES STEPHEN WALKER	GATESVILLE
WILLIAM PENN WINCHESTER	WACO

FEBRUARY 12, 1935.

The dedication on February 12, 1935, of a bridge built across the tracks in Round Rock was the occasion for the unveiling of a State Highway Commission plaque on which a brief statement and the ten victims' names were embossed. Photograph by Todd Copeland.

In addition to such public memorials, every Baylor student who has bought an official class ring since 1995 wears a tribute to the Immortal Ten. The ring includes the depiction of a railroad spike, located on one side of the band, to symbolize the lost students.

In 1996, Baylor's senior class elected to apply its class gift toward a set of statues that would finally give the memory of the Immortal Ten a prominent presence on campus. "We felt it was time something was done to honor their memories," said Chase Palmer, the permanent president of the Class of 1996 and an attorney in

Marshall. "If you're going to call it a tradition, you ought to do something about it."

Subsequent senior classes followed suit, with students contributing their $100 general university deposits toward the proposed memorial, but that practice ended after Baylor stopped requiring students to make the deposit. In the spring of 2001, Baylor's Student Congress allocated $10,000 from the Student Life Fund for the statues. However, by May 2006 the funds collected for the project still fell considerably short of the $280,000 estimated total cost. That was when the Baylor Chamber of Commerce and the Baylor Alumni Association each pledged $50,000 to bring about the project's completion

Sculptor Bruce Greene, shown here in his Clifton studio, was commissioned to create the memorial to the Immortal Ten for installation in the center of Baylor's campus. The memorial consists of ten life-size bronze statues. Six of the students are depicted in bas-relief in a ten-by-eight-foot panel. The other four students—Robert Hannah Jr., James Walker, Ivey Foster Jr., and Clyde "Abe" Kelley—are represented by freestanding figures. Photograph by Rod Aydelotte.

during the months leading up to the accident's eightieth anniversary, on January 22, 2007.

The set of intricately detailed bronze statues, prominently located in the center of campus, was created by Clifton sculptor Bruce Greene. It consists of ten life-size figures, with six of them depicted in bas-relief in a ten-by-eight-foot panel. Three more freestanding figures — representing Robert Hannah Jr., James Walker, and Ivey Foster Jr. — form a second row, while the tenth, representing Clyde "Abe" Kelley, stands alone in front, a basketball held against his hip.

The scale of the memorial is certainly grand, but what message do Palmer and the project's other planners hope the memorial conveys? "We'd like people to understand that just because you're young doesn't mean you're guaranteed a place on this earth forever," he said. "What I get from the story is the message of a sacrifice of self for others, represented by Abe Kelley, and that life is precious, so take advantage of your opportunities and live each day as if it were your last."

In Round Rock, an initiative to honor the Immortal Ten has been proceeding independently of Baylor's memorial project. The city's Historic Preserva-tion Commission has proposed the development of a memorial park on city-owned land near the site of the bus-train collision. Plans currently call for the park to be connected to the Lake Creek Trail that will run past the municipal office complex. In addition, local officials are applying for an official state marker from the Texas State Historical Commission to mark the crash site. They hope to pair it with the Texas State Highway Commission's 1935 plaque.

ACKNOWLEDGMENTS AND
SOURCE NOTES

I would like to thank the following people who provided support in researching and writing this story or who supplied information, through personal interviews, used in the narrative: Nina Murray Kendrick, sister of Willis Murray; John Curry, nephew of Willis Murray; Martha Gooch Hendrick, daughter of Ed Gooch; Alice Cheavens Baird, daughter of Dave Cheavens; Duke Slade, son of Louis Slade; Will Paradeaux, nephew of Louis Slade; Robert Strickland, son of Keifer Strickland; Shelby Strickland, nephew of Keifer Strickland; Jon Washam, son of Weir Washam; Jim Washam, son of Weir Washam; Helen Hailey Ligon, former business professor at Baylor and niece of Robert Hailey; James Powell, nephew of James Walker; Charles Baxter, 1930 Baylor graduate; Katie Reynolds Sheffield, 1926 Baylor graduate; MariLee Baird, 1930 Baylor graduate; Mary Kemendo Sendón, 1922 Baylor graduate; Maurine Couch Burleson, 1929 Baylor graduate; McDonald

"Don" Held, 1933 Baylor graduate, whose freshman football team was coached by Weir Washam; Pat Groner, 1941 Baylor graduate, whose brother, Ed "Dutch" Groner, was Jack Castellaw's roommate; M. L. "Hub" Northen, Baylor student from 1925 to 1929; Marion Mathis "Barney" Hale, Baylor student and football player from 1925 to 1929; Thornton Sterling, 1936 Baylor graduate; Lisa Asher, Meg Cullar, and Judy Prather, members of the *Baylor Line*'s staff; the governing board and executive leadership of the Baylor Alumni Association; Ellen Kuniyuki Brown and Kent Keeth from The Texas Collection at Baylor University; Thomas Turner, former assistant to Baylor President Abner McCall; Neal Knighton; Chase Palmer; Eugene Baker, former Baylor historian; WJ Wimpee, former Baylor chaplain; Robert Reid, former professor of history at Baylor; Vince Clark; James Vardaman, former professor of history at Baylor; Frank Leavell, former professor of English at Baylor; Karen Thompson, Round Rock historian; and Dave Campbell, former sports editor of the *Waco Tribune-Herald*.

In addition to interviews, the factual details and quotations used in the narrative were drawn from a variety of primary sources: Hannah-Wiley Family Papers, The Texas Collection, Baylor University; Samuel Palmer Brooks Papers, The Texas Collection; Immortal Ten scrapbooks, The Texas Collection; *Daily Lariat*, January 21–February 6, 1927; *Waco Times-Herald*, January 21–26, 1927; *Waco News-Tribune*, January 23–24, 1927; *Taylor Daily Press*, January 22, 1927; *Dallas Morning News*, January 23–25, 1927; *Fort Worth Star-Telegram*, January 23, 1927; *The Daily Texan*, January 23, 1927;

The New York Times, January 23, 1927; *Baylor Monthly*, February 1927; written opinions in the *Wesley Bradshaw v. Baylor University et al.* lawsuit (Court of Civil Appeals of Texas, June 27, 1932; Supreme Court of Texas, July 17, 1935); *Baylor Round-Up*, 1922–31; *Baylor*, February–March, 1984; "Bravery at Baylor," by Kent Keeth, *The Baylor Line*, November 1976; *Waco Tribune-Herald*, November 8, 1980; *King Football: Greatest Moments in Texas High School Football History*, 2003; and obituaries of crash survivors as published in various publications over the years. Information used in the appendix on the Freshman Mass Meeting was drawn from several sources listed above as well as the *Baylor Lariat*, 1928–1986. Information used in the appendix on memorials to the Immortal Ten was drawn from several sources listed above, as well as "Toward Greater Safety," by Charles Simons, *Texas Parade*, November 1937.